Advance Praise for Blue Chips & Hot Tips

Howard M. Schilit is "a particularly astute analyst of Initial Public Offerings [and] an expert on corporate financial games."

> Louis Rukeyser
> **Syndicated Columnist and**
> **TV Personality**

"The most useful primer on the subject I've ever read."

> Michael F. Holland
> **Chairman & CEO**
> **Salomon Asset Manage-**
> **ment Inc.**

"BLUE CHIPS & HOT TIPS ... provides an outstanding layman's guide to the IPO world. By identifying the common denominators of successful IPOs, as well as the factors that signal potential failure, it gives investors the tools to select the winners and avoid the losers.... By doing his homework and following the evaluation techniques described in this well researched book, [the individual investor] can ... significantly imporve the odds of finding a sound opportunity with the potential for substantial upside."

> Mary C. Farrell,
> **Investment Strategist**
> **First Vice President**
> **PaineWebber Incorporated**

"What could be hard to understand is made easy...I have 30 years experience as a business man and entrepreneur, and have been investing in the stock market for 10 years. This book has brought into focus so many things about running and investing in a business. Wish I had read it 20 years ago."

Howard M. Arnold
Entrepreneur and CEO
Founder of Sage Systems
and Chartway Technologies

This book deals with a "timely topic in today's financial markets...I am particularly concerned about the retail investor separating the wheat from the chaff...[This] book will be very helpful to both the institutional and retail investor as they plow through the hundreds of IPO prospectuses that have been issued this year...The 'Turnons' and 'Turnoffs' section was particularly appropriate."

D. Jonathan Merriman
President
Curhan, Merriman Capital
Management, Inc.

BLUE CHIPS & HOT TIPS

Identifying Emerging Growth Companies Most Likely to Succeed

W. Keith Schilit, Ph.D.

Howard M. Schilit, Ph.D., CPA

New York Institute of Finance

New York London Toronto Sydney Tokyo Singapore

Prentice-Hall International (UK) Limited, *London*
Prentice-Hall of Australia Pty. Limited, *Sydney*
Prentice-Hall Canada, Inc., *Toronto*
Prentice-Hall Hispanoamericana, S.A., *Mexico*
Prentice-Hall of India Private Limited, *New Delhi*
Prentice-Hall of Japan, Inc., *Tokyo*
Simon & Schuster Asia Pte. Ltd., *Singapore*
Editora Prentice-Hall do Brasil, Ltda., *Rio de Janeiro*

© 1992 by

W. Keith Schilit
Howard M. Schilit

10 9 8 7 6 5 4 3 2

Library of Congress Cataloging-in-Publication Data

Schilit, W. Keith
Blue chips & hot tips : identifying emerging growth companies most
likely to succeed / W. Keith Schilit, Howard M. Schilit.
p. cm.
Includes index.
ISBN 0-13-089442-7
1. Investment analysis. 2. Stocks. I. Schilit Howard M.
II. Title. III. Title: Blue chips and hot tips.
HG4529.S37   1992
332.63'2044–dc20   91-45229
                                                CIP

ISBN 0-13-089442-7

Printed in the United States of America

To three generations of Schilits:

- **Our parents, Ethel and Irving**
- **Our wives, Diane and Karen**
  Our siblings, Audrey and Rob
- **Our children, Jonathan, Suzanne, Amy, and Jordan**

About the Authors

The authors are founders of the Center for Financial Research and Analysis [CFRA]*, which conducts research and analysis on emerging growth companies. It also publishes an authoritative research report on new issues entitled *IPO Research Digest*.

Howard M. Schilit, Ph.D., CPA

Howard M. Schilit is a noted financial statement analyst, expert accounting witness, and lecturer. He has written and taught seminars on a variety of topics including: valuing closely-held businesses, finding red flags on financial statements, finding early warning signals in reading a prospectus, and assessing the quality of earnings.

He is an Associate Professor of Accounting and the Director of Graduate Programs in Accounting at The American University in Washington, D.C. In addition to teaching courses on financial statement analysis, he has done extensive research and published articles related to the valuation of businesses and initial public offerings.

As a consultant, Dr. Schilit serves frequently as an "accounting expert" in court and arbitration proceedings, representing the U.S. Department of Justice, NCR Corporation, and others. In addition, he has served as the lead financial statement analyst and the author of a financial analysis software program for Federal Filings, Inc., a Washington-based electronic financial newswire (a subsidiary of Dow Jones).

He holds an M.S. in Accounting from the State University of New York (SUNY) at Binghamton and an M.B.A. and Ph.D. in Accounting from the University of Maryland. He is also a CPA in the State of Maryland.

---

* Center for Financial Research and Analysis
  10800 Mazwood Place
  Rockville, Maryland 20852
  (301) 530-8224

W. Keith Schilit, Ph.D.

W. Keith Schilit is an accomplished author, consultant, entrepreneur, and lecturer. He has written approximately three dozen articles on such topics as investing in emerging growth companies, analyzing initial public offerings, starting and financing new business ventures, preparing business plans, raising venture capital, strategic planning, and general management, and has given numerous talks to corporations, associations, and universities on these topics. He is the author of two recent books on venture capital (both published by Prentice Hall): *The Entrepreneur's Guide to Preparing a Winning Businees Plan & Raising Venture Capital* and *Dream Makers & Deal Breakers: Inside the Venture Capital Industry.*

He has been a consultant and has conducted training programs for numerous businesses and has served as an expert witness in the area of corporate valuation. His clients have included: The U.S. Civil Service Commission, Niagara Mohawk Power, Corning Glass Works, National Tire Dealers and Retreaders Association, Robbins Manufacturing, Medcross, and Assix International.

He has founded three businesses and has assisted in the start-up of several others. He is currently president of Catalyst Ventures (Tampa, FL), a consulting firm which assists small-growth businesses.

He is a founding member of the Strategic Management Society, an international society of over 1,000 consultants, executives, and academicians. He has been a director of several corporations and community groups.

Dr. Schilit, who holds an M.B.A. and Ph.D. in strategic planning from the University of Maryland, has served on the faculties of Keio University (in Tokyo) and Syracuse University, and is currently on the faculty of the University of South Florida (in Tampa).

Acknowledgments

Several people helped us in many important ways on this book and we express our sincere appreciation:

Samuel A. Dedio, financial analyst at Standard & Poor's and formerly graduate student at The American University provided invaluable research support, particularly in preparing the graphs.

Dr. Robert L. Losey, professor of finance at The American University, was the creative genius behind the book's title.

Robert P. Schilit, economist and freelance writer, offered valuable suggestions in editing the manuscript.

Diane Lipson Schilit provided outstanding assistance in proofreading the manuscript.

Neill Brownstein, General Partner, Bessemer Venture Partners, offered insightful comments in reviewing a draft of the book.

Introduction

Several years ago, one of our good friends was fortunate enough to hear Sam Walton address a group of retailers. He was so enthused by his remarks that when Walton's company, Wal-Mart, went public in 1970, he invested $1,000 in this little known discount retailing chain. Today, that $1,000 investment is worth over half a million dollars.

We frequently hear similar stories of other small investors who were fortunate enough to invest in such companies as Home Depot (which increased in value by over 7,000%—or 70-fold—over the decade of the 1980s), Liz Claiborne (up 3,400% over that time period), Adobe Systems (up 1,600%), LA Gear (up 1,400%), or Autodesk (up 1,200%) at the time—or shortly after—these companies went public. Such investments have enabled these investors to become million-aires, solely as a result of their intelligent investment decisions.

To put in some perspective the magnitude of success these companies have achieved, consider the following. Turn the clock back about ten years, long before most investors knew about Liz Claiborne's line of clothing. You, as a value oriented shopper, how-ever, were thrilled with their clothing so you went on a mini-shopping spree and bought the following Liz Claiborne items at a local women's clothing store:

6 suits @ $200	$1,200
6 dresses @ $150	900
8 blouses @ $50	400
6 pairs of pants @ $50	300
4 pairs of shoes @ $75	300
Assorted accessories	400
TOTAL	$3,500

After tidying up your wardrobe, you decided that it was time to tidy up your house. So you paid a visit to the local Home Depot to pick up a few items for those much needed repairs around the house. Here's what you purchased:

Kitchen cabinets	$ 300
Floor tile for kitchen	500
Paint and wallpaper	300
4 light fixtures @ $100	400
2 door units @ $300	600
Utility shed	300
Lumber for fence and deck	400
Plants for landscaping	600
Patio furniture	500
TOTAL	$3,900

Certainly, today, ten years later, your Liz Claiborne clothing would be worn out and your house would need additional repairs. However, if instead of spending the $3,900 at the Home Depot store, you had invested that amount in its stock, your $3,900 investment would have appreciated enough by now to buy a $1/4 million house, without even having to take out a mortgage. And if instead of indulging yourself with the $3,500 of Liz Claiborne clothing, you had invested that same amount in its stock, today you would have enough cash to build a $100,000 addition to that home, with plenty of money left over to fill your closets with plenty of Liz Claiborne outfits, not to mention a few designer originals!

Why do some emerging growth companies prosper and reward their investors with outstanding returns while others fail to match their early expectations? In 1989, we began a groundbreaking study of the most successful and least successful emerging growth companies of the last two decades, with the intent of identifying characteristics common to each group. The results are summarized in *Blue Chips & Hot Tips.*

From our analysis of scores of emerging growth companies, we have identified those key factors which differentiated the winners from the losers. This guide is filled with suggestions and strategies to help investors spot the early signs of success and failure. By following the framework outlined in *Blue Chips & Hot Tips*, investors will be able to identify investment opportunities most likely to succeed and to avoid those which are most likely to fail. It will be clear from the examples cited throughout this book that our approach is based on sound research and analysis which has been proven to enhance investment performance in emerging growth companies. Yet, it is presented in a simplified (but not overly simplistic), easy-to-follow manner that will benefit all investors, from the novice to the experienced investor.

While *Blue Chips & Hot Tips* can be classified as an investment guide, unlike other investment books, it incorporates *strategic analysis* into traditional *financial analysis*. Typical investment books focus almost exclusively on mechanical procedures that form the basis of financial analysis — either *fundamental analysis* (based on historical financial statements) or *technical analysis* (based primarily on trends in stock price behavior). On the other hand, typical management books focus almost exclusively on such strategic factors as a company's product or service, its management team, or its strategic position in an industry. This book is different from these others in a profound way. Because of the unique backgrounds of the two authors (one of us is trained as a financial analyst and is adept in analyzing financial statements, while the other one is trained in the area of strategic management), our approach to analyzing emerging growth companies combines our different backgrounds and expertise and blends the most current approaches from both traditional financial analysis and traditional strategic analysis. So, *Blue Chips & Hot Tips* certainly goes beyond the basics of analyzing financial statements. It also includes many important management lessons, which can be valuable for entrepreneurs and managers of emerging growth companies interested in following a model of successful companies.

We've identified several dozen *turnons* and *turnoffs* by examining four broad categories of predictive factors — product/market, management and organization, financial position, and financial arrangement. Among our most significant conclusions and recommendations, which will be discussed at length throughout the book are the following:

- Look for companies that have a focus that is clearly defined
- Cherish a company with a proprietary technology
- Notice that low tech companies can have significant competitive advantages
- Beware of "hot" stocks in "hot" industries
- Note that management is more important than the technology
- Note that prominent venture capitalists as directors can strengthen the company significantly
- Watch for quality and quantity of related party transactions
- Search for companies with strong earnings and earnings growth
- Look beyond net income; beware of shrinking profit margins
- Look for "quality of earnings"
- Use the balance sheet to predict future earnings
- Watch for unusual or unexplained increases in accounts receivable or inventory
- Monitor the debt/equity ratio
- Be cautious of companies that fail to generate enough cash to fuel their growth
- Search for companies that use the proceeds from an offering to foster future growth
- Look for companies which have already received substantial funding, especially from established venture capitalists
- Watch for those companies with outrageous valuations

Contents

PART ONE

Turnons and *Turnoffs*

CHAPTER 1

Watch Out
for Buffalo Chips

================================

RISK AND RETURN

There's ample evidence to demonstate that the greatest returns for investors often result from investing in emerging growth companies at the time the companies went public. Those investors who bought shares in Xerox, The Limited, Liz Claiborne, or Microsoft at their *initial public offerings* (IPOs) have earned phenomenal returns. However, this should not mask the substantial risk of investing in IPOs. As the investors in ZZZZ Best, Kaypro, or Genex have learned, early stage investments can lead to staggering losses.

Anyone who has taken an introductory finance course has been exposed to the notion of *risk and return*; that is, investments that provide an opportunity for substantial returns, tend to be rather risky. This is certainly apparent in studying the performance of small young public companies, some of which have performed exceedingly well while others have been major disappointments. Interestingly, the average returns for such investments have been substantially below those of well-established "blue chip" companies. In a recent *Forbes*

3

magazine survey of almost 2,000 companies that "went public" during the 1980s, 71% did worse than the overall stock market (as measured by the S & P 500 Index), with an average performance relative to the overall market of –19%.[1] By 1990, more than half of those new issues were worth less than at their initial offering price, one-third of those companies were valued at less than half of their initial offering price, and 6% of the total went bankrupt. But, oh, have there been winners! Imagine if you had invested in such companies as Liz Claiborne, Home Depot, Adobe, Compaq Computer or Microsoft at the time they went public. The returns on these companies would have more than offset dozens of losers.

IN A RECENT SURVEY OF COMPANIES THAT "WENT PUBLIC" DURING THE 1980S, 71% DID WORSE THAN THE OVERALL STOCK MARKET, WITH AN AVERAGE PERFORMANCE RELATIVE TO THE OVERALL MARKET OF –19%.

WHAT THIS BOOK IS ABOUT

This book is a guide for investing in emerging growth businesses. It focuses on the "new issues"—i.e., those emerging ventures that have recently "gone public" or are about to go public via an IPO.

Of course, we're all familiar with the term *blue chips*, which are those established companies such as Coca-Cola, General Electric, Johnson & Johnson, Procter & Gamble, and 3M that have provided investors with strong, stable returns over many years. This book does not focus on the blue chips, although it does identify the blue chips of the *future*. Rather, it focuses on the *red chips*, those hot, emerging growth companies—such as Compaq, Microsoft, LA Gear—that are generally higher in risk, but often higher in return and in excitement— than the "blue chips." It also examines the *buffalo chips*, which, as the name would imply, should be avoided at all costs. In short, this book

---

[1] Steven Ramos & Steve Kichen. "Long Shots and Small Returns." *Forbes*, June 25, 1990, pg. 273ff.

tells how to pick the *red chips* (i.e., the stars of tomorrow) and how to avoid the *buffalo chips*.

There are countless books written about investments that promise to tell you "how to get rich quick." This book is very different. We use solidly grounded research techniques to provide a framework to assist the investor in using public information readily available to make more intelligent investment decisions. Although our research employs sophisticated techniques, we have translated our findings into a language and a format that any investor, from the novice to the professional, can easily read, enjoy, and apply. Of course, we like to follow Will Rogers' advice on investing:

> Don't gamble: Take all your savings and buy some good stock and hold it 'til it goes up, then sell it. If it don't (sic) go up, don't buy it.

OBJECTIVES OF THE BOOK

Because of the exciting high return/high risk nature of emerging growth companies, we began investigating whether there were measurable characteristics which differentiated the most successful from the least successful ones. If we could identify such factors, then any investor who uses these characteristics as a guide could reduce the risk, while earning higher returns, in investing in exciting growth companies.

The purpose of this book is to share our research findings on emerging growth companies with you, and to demonstrate how you can improve your investment performance by following the framework that we have developed. This framework is easy to follow and takes a minimal amount of time to apply.

Listening To Professionals

One conclusion that we've reached, after spending years listening to professional investors, is not to rely on them. Individual investors in IPOs and small emerging growth companies may be "fortunate," in a sense, because professionals rarely follow these companies. As a result, the professionals often begin recommending these high growth companies when it's too late. Consider The Limited, one of the superstar stock performers of recent years. The company went public in 1969, yet it wasn't until 1974 that an analyst from a major brokerage firm (First Boston) began to follow the company. Then it wasn't until 1975, when The Limited already had 100 stores in operation and after the stock had already appreciated significantly, that the first institutional investor (T. Rowe Price) bought stock in the company. By 1981, having already grown to 400 stores, The Limited still had only six analysts following its stock. In 1985, analysts began to take a more careful look and institutions began buying the stock aggressively. Unfortunately for them, the institutions were buying the stock aggressively *at just the wrong time,* when it was at its high and overvalued significantly. Not surprisingly, the professional analysts missed the entire party, and, of course, those investors who followed their advice, also missed out.

While we don't wish to criticize or denigrate the outstanding performance of such legendary investment professionals as Peter Lynch, John Templeton, Warren Buffet, John Neff, George Soros, and others, we do assert (and they would agree) that their success is based on evaluating information that is *readily available to all of us.* These outstanding stock-pickers are successful, not because they rely solely on sophisticated statistical models, rather because they are alert to clues all around them. For example, Peter Lynch, formerly the head of Fidelity Magellan's hugely successful equity fund, loves to give his wife credit for discovering L'Eggs, one of his best-performing investments. Likewise, it didn't take complex mathematical models using high-powered computers to forecast that Wal-Mart, Toys "R" Us, The Limited, Home Depot, and the like, would be great investments; all it took was a Saturday afternoon drive to the nearest mall or shopping center.

Of course, spotting a potential success story—like Toys "R" Us or Apple Computer—simply by noticing its product or shopping at one of its stores, is *only the starting point* in selecting an investment. You need a way to differentiate a Toys "R" Us from a Coleco, or an Apple Computer from a Vector Graphic. That is where more analysis by the investor is needed, and that is where this book will help.

It certainly would be unfair to conclude that professional investors fail to provide an important service. For individual investors, especially those with limited resources or time—mutual funds are a low risk, low excitement, trouble-free way to invest. However, investors who are willing to spend some time doing some fairly unsophisticated analysis, can create returns significantly better than most in the realm of mutual funds.

Using Our Framework

By using our framework, your results can be dramatic and rewarding financially. If you had applied this framework in the past, you would have been alerted to the almost unlimited growth and profit potential of some of the most successful emerging growth companies in recent years, as well as to the early indicators of disaster of some of the least successful ones.

Our model identified such companies as Microsoft, Liz Claiborne, Compaq, and Home Depot as potential winners. Moreover, it identified such companies as Worlds of Wonder, Genex, DeLaurentiis Entertainment, Vector Graphic, and Columbia Data Products as potential losers through which investors would have lost fortunes. An important question to consider is: Were there early warning signs at the time these companies went public that would have alerted investors to stay away? The answer is *yes*. We have found certain key factors that have alerted us to potential trouble. Any investor who has used our model then, would have found those same warning signals.

WHO WILL BENEEFIT FROM READING THIS BOOK?

This book will be helpful for: 1. *individual investors*; 2. *managers* at emerging growth companies which may be planning to go public; and 3. *investment professionals* who assist emerging growth companies in their growth, in process of raising capital especially.

Individual investors: Any solid research that helps investors reduce their risk and increase their rewards is certainly valuable. While our research has focused on IPOs primarily, our approach can be applied to other equity investments, as well. As we illustrate in our chapter on analyzing financial statements (Chapter 6), our rules on evaluating the *quality of earnings* and the *valuation* of a company also apply to analyses of *established companies*. In addition, our framework would benefit those who analyze—or may wish to invest in—smaller, *privately-held businesses*. In fact, this book is a direct outgrowth of two previous books by one of the authors on venture capital investments.[2]

---

[2] Refer to the following two recent books by W. Keith Schilit: *The Entrepreneur's Guide to Preparing a Winning Business Plan & Raising Venture Capital* (Prentice Hall, 1990); *Dream Makers & Deal Breakers: Inside the Venture Capital Industry* (Prentice Hall, 1991)

Managers at emerging growth companies: A young, successful company often "dreams" of one day going public. If it plans for that day carefully and is aware of pitfalls common to those companies which were unsuccessful, then it may *avoid* their mistakes. For example, an early stage, privately-held genetic engineering company planning to go public over the next year or two could benefit if it knew those characteristics common to other successful and unsuccessful genetic engineering companies, which had gone public. Consider two actual genetic engineering companies which went public in the early 1980s—Genentech and Genex. Over the years, Genentech has become a star performer, while Genex has become a major disappointment. By studying the key factors *differentiating* Genentech from Genex, managers at our hypothetical company would be wise to model their facility after Genentech, rather than Genex.

Investment professionals: Underwriters, lawyers, and accountants play key roles in assisting clients and in preparing them for public (and private) offerings. These investment professionals can benefit by knowing the major risk factors common to those emerging growth companies that had significantly "underperformed" the broader stock market. Recently, risks to the professional have apparently increased. Consider that Donald Hebb Jr. recently stepped down as president of the brokerage firm Alex Brown & Sons amidst some highly publicized problems with IPOs the firm had underwritten. Two of these losing new issues were In-Store Advertising and Silk Greenhouse, both of which lost most of their value shortly after going public. Another problem facing professionals is that investors who lose substantial amounts of money from their investments in IPOs have brought suit against their underwriters, attorneys, and accountants. This was the case with ZZZZ Best and Crazy Eddie. Likewise, shareholders of Smith Corona filed suit against its financial advisors after seeing their investment plummet 77% after going public. Whenever a stock offering is unsuccessful and investors suffer substantial losses, the advisors (underwriters, lawyers, and accountants) are often held accountable by angry investors. In our litigious society, financial and legal advisors to any publicly traded company would certainly benefit by knowing the high risk factors of their clients.

WHY THIS BOOK IS NEEDED

How can you reduce your risk when investing in emerging growth companies? Where can you obtain reliable, objective, and independent information about the quality of these young companies? Of course, there is much information available, most of which is provided by financial advisers or "stock-pickers." (The SEC, however, imposes a 90 day "quiet period" for IPOs, which prohibits the underwriter from disseminating any information about the new issues during this time period, other than through the prospectus of the company.) Unfortunately, these advisors often work for investment firms that have a financial incentive to sell securities to investors and, as a result, may lack total objectivity and independence.

Recently, the issue of independence of financial advisors has been elevated to front page news. In March of 1990, for example, shortly before Donald Trump's crown jewel "Taj Mahal" casino was about to open, Marvin Roffman, a veteran securities analyst at the brokerage firm Janney Montgomery Scott, wrote a critical report, questioning the long term prospects of the casino. Mr. Trump, incensed by the report, threatened to sue Janney Montgomery for libel if the analyst was not immediately fired or if a retraction was not forthcoming. When Mr. Roffman refused to retract his comments, Janney Montgomery Scott fired him.

As events unfolded, Roffman was correct in questioning Trump's cash flow projections needed by the Taj Mahal to meet its huge debt. (We all later learned that Trump came perilously close to defaulting on some of his loans.) What troubled us, along with many others, was that an analyst or (in this case) the head of a securities firm could "knuckle under" the pressure of a big client, resulting in biased recommendations for investors. This episode has raised some serious questions about the independence of analysts and of brokerage firms, and *this should concern investors*. Congressional consumer-advocate Representative John Dingell was outraged by this incident, and has made the following statement:

> [It] raises serious questions about honesty and integrity of Wall Street research.

Obviously, the lack of independence would have tremendous implications for the individual investor who relies on the reports of analysts in making investment decisions. According to one observer, there is an unwritten understanding on Wall Street "not to make negative recommendations—or at least not to make them too loudly." Certainly, an investor should be concerned about any lack of balance in reporting a company's news. Most analysts' reports are intended for investors to *buy* stock, rather than *sell* stock; this clearly helps generate additional commissions for brokers, but unfortunately may hurt investors. As noted by one analyst,

> A 'buy' is more sexy [than a 'sell']. [Brokers] can call everyone who owns [the stock], and everyone who doesn't.

This notion was confirmed by Zacks Investment Research Inc., in their survey of 1,500 companies which showed that less than 10% of all recommendations were *sells*. Thus, in 90% of research reports by brokerage firms, the recommendation was "positive" or "neutral." Why aren't there more sell recommendations by analysts, especially when there is so much *negative* news on deteriorating earnings and a weakening economy?

IN A SURVEY OF 1,500 COMPANIES, LESS THAN 10% OF ALL RECOMMENDATIONS WERE SELLS.

OUR APPROACH OR FRAMEWORK

From the above examples, it becomes obvious that a void exists for investors who need independent, objective, and accurate information on investment opportunities and, in particular, on emerging growth companies. In essence, the individual investor is on his or her own when it comes to such investments. Our goal is to fill that void and to demonstrate an approach or a framework which *investors can use* in doing their own analysis. This book introduces you to this framework and tells you how to use it to improve your investment decisions. The framework is designed to *control the risk* and to highlight the key factors which are predictive of successful and unsuccessful investments.

Regardless of the framework used, we realize that any time you attempt to predict future events—which is what stock picking or forecasting is all about—you *will* be wrong on many occasions. Obviously, the riskier the investment (such as IPOs and other early-stage investments that are the subject of this book), the more difficult it is to be "on target" consistently. However, this book provides a set of carefully researched, easy-to-follow rules to assist you in selecting successful emerging growth companies, while avoiding unsuccessful ones. These rules are designed to reduce your risk, without reducing the returns on (or the fun you'll have making), those investments. Most important, the rules are designed to weed out the losers—or *buffalo chips*—from the winners—or *red chips*. In knowing what characteristics to look for, an investor in emerging growth ventures should be more selective, and, ultimately, more successful in picking long-term winners.

Our framework, which we refer to as *low risk speculation*, offers an objective, unbiased approach for investing in emerging ventures. The approach is based on our thorough analysis of companies that have gone public over the past two decades. Contrary to what some investors think, our research has shown that investing in early stage companies is not a "crap shoot." Rather, it takes skill to find the "gems." Through our extensive research efforts, we have been able to identify those characteristics which *differentiate* the successful emerging growth companies from the unsuccessful ones. By knowing what factors to examine, any investor can successfully use this approach to identify which investments have the greatest likelihood of success, compared to those with the greatest likelihood of failure.

> *OUR RESEARCH HAS SHOWN THAT INVESTING IN EARLY STAGE COMPANIES IS NOT A "CRAP SHOOT." RATHER, IT TAKES SKILL TO FIND THE "GEMS."*

It has been said that the difference between an *investor* and a *speculator* is that an investor buys stocks that go up and a speculator buys stocks that go down. We'll try to make investors out of you. In the process, we'll recount some interesting, and often entertaining stories about many people and companies with which you may be quite familiar. Of course, there's always an element of risk associated with these investments. As Mark Twain once said,

> October is one of the particularly dangerous months to speculate on stocks. The others are July, January, September, April, November, May, March, June, December, August, and February.

Patience Is a Virtue

Perhaps a buddy of yours bought 100 shares of some early stage, high tech company (let's call it HiTech Corporation), when it went public in 1983 or so. As the Dow Jones Industrial Index increased by more than 1000 points over the ensuing months in the midst of a raging *bull market* (i.e., increasing stock prices), HiTech doubled or even tripled in value. The big question is, where is HiTech today? If it's like many of the other, hyped technology stocks of the early 1980s, then it has faded into oblivion.

It is important to recognize that several factors, aside from the quality of a company, can affect the performance of a stock, at least over the short term. For young companies, such factors as emotion, greed, hype, and so forth, can certainly play a substantial role in pushing the price of a high-profile, albeit poorly managed company, to unheard of levels. Just like emotion can drive up the price of a stock, so it can drive its price down, and often more rapidly. Consider Silk Greenhouse, which doubled within months of its IPO, only to lose 90% of its value over the following year or so.

We view an investment in an IPO or any other emerging venture as a *long-term investment* in a young company before it has experienced most of its growth. Our intent is to identify which companies will be the "winners" and "losers" of the coming decade. We attempt to identify quality companies that are likely to perform at high levels over the long term; our approach ignores short-term fluctuations, which may be affected by many factors other than the fundamentals of a particular company. For example, the stock price of many outstanding companies plummeted following Iraq's invasion of Kuwait in August, 1990. Our model ignores such short-term fluctuations and instead, identifies factors that can predict which companies will most likely be successful or unsuccessful over the years.

How to Succeed As An Investor

Investors are generally successful for two main reasons: 1. they pick securities which are *undervalued*; and 2. they avoid securities which are *overvalued*. Although both are important, most approaches to investing emphasize the former only. We, however, place considerable emphasis on the latter. By limiting the risks or red flags inherent in many emerging growth companies, you can improve your overall long-term investment performance considerably.

INVESTORS ARE SUCCESSFUL BECAUSE THEY PICK SECURITIES WHICH ARE UNDERVALUED *AND AVOID SECURITIES WHICH ARE* OVER-VALUED.

Our approach to low risk speculation focuses primarily on searching for negatives—that is, the red flags. Thus, we look for early signs of a potential problem. When we find any important red flags, we are alerted to avoid buying such companies. Unlike those analysts (that we previously mentioned) who recommended a buy or a hold in 90% of the cases, we take a more *cautious* approach and search for *early warning signals* of significant problems, which might suggest that the investor sell or avoid buying a particular company.

OUR APPROACH TO LOW RISK SPECULATION FOCUSES PRIMARILY ON SEARCHING FOR NEGATIVES—THAT IS, THE RED FLAGS. *THUS, WE LOOK FOR EARLY SIGNS OF A POTENTIAL PROBLEM.*

While buying emerging growth companies certainly is riskier than investing in established blue chip companies, it is still desirable to take a conservative position to limit your risk. Thus, our goal in highlighting potential problems in emerging growth companies is to help you limit your risk. In so doing, you can avoid buying overvalued stocks and sell stocks prior to a major decline.

Our fundamental belief is that almost anyone could take advantage of this approach. We have found that it does not require any special training to use our approach. Rather, we feel that any investor who uses our framework should be able to improve his or her record in selecting "winners" and in avoiding "losers."

STRUCTURE OF THE BOOK

The chapters in this book are structured around the *predictive factors* that we've identified from our research. These are the factors which differentiate winning from losing investments. Our style is conversational, and we share stories about the top-performing and worst-performing emerging growth businesses of the past two decades.

Based on our research, we have identified a number of *positive predictive factors*—those common to the successful IPOs, and have identified a number of *negative predictive factors*—those common to the unsuccessful IPOs. Each chapter in Part II of this book focuses on an important predictive factor and provides illustrations of companies that have either exhibited or lacked those characteristics.

The third part of the book entitled *Tomorrow's Winners and Losers* demonstrates how our framework can be used for investment decisions *today* in predicting the "stars" of tomorrow. In this section, we make extensive use of historical information to support our model. As we have learned from philosopher George Santayana: "the future is where we are condemned to repeat what we fail to remember of the past."

CHAPTER 2

Yesterday's Red Chips ...Today's Blue Chips

GATEWAY TECHNOLOGY: YESTERDAY'S RED CHIP

In 1982, Gateway Technology, a Houston-based microcomputer manufacturer hoping to obtain start-up capital, contacted Sevin Rosen Management, the noted venture capital firm. Gateway, like many similar companies manufacturing IBM-compatible computers, presented the venture capitalists with some optimistic sales projections for the coming years. Ben Rosen, a general partner of Sevin Rosen, and one of the most respected venture capitalists in the country, had trouble believing Gateway's first year sales projections of $35 million and its second year projections of $198 million. Nonetheless, Rosen saw a capable management team, and decided to invest in Gateway Technology.

Follow Up on Gateway

Whatever became of Gateway? First, don't get thrown by the name. If you are not familiar with the name Gateway or if you are not using a "Gateway" computer today, it's because Gateway changed its name to "Compaq." Of course, Compaq is familiar to all of us; it's one of the few successful computer companies that began in the early to mid 1980s that not only survived the decade, but became one of the most successful and admired corporations in this country.

Let's take a look at the numbers. Compaq easily surpassed its projection of $35 million and generated a *phenomenal* $111 million of revenues during its *first* full year of business (a record, at that time, for a start-up), and $329 million in its second year, thereby surpassing its own optimistic sales projections. And Sevin Rosen was rewarded for its faith in the company aptly; its $2.5 million investment grew to $38 million or 15-fold by the time Compaq went public nine short months later.

Just how well has Compaq Computer done over the years? By 1989, Compaq generated nearly $3 billion in revenues. Moreover, although Compaq was still a fairly new company, in a recent survey it had become recognized as among the best managed *Fortune* 500 companies in this country. According to Goldman Sachs computer analyst Daniel Benton, who was quoted recently in *Dun's Business Month*:

> Compaq is a case study in management excellence. It is the only company in the world that has established a brand name better than IBM's.

Those individual investors who purchased Compaq at the time of its IPO and held onto their investment would have gleaned a 5-fold appreciation in stock price over a six-year period. Of course, the earlier stage investors, those who invested in Compaq before it went public, did even better; the value of Sevin Rosen's original $2.5 million investment in 1982 is now worth over $1/4 billion, a 100-fold increase.

PREDICTING SUCCESS AND FAILURE

While it is interesting to recount the success story of Compaq Computer, it would have been far more rewarding financially to have invested in it at its initial public offering. Might you have forecasted that Compaq would have been so successful? Might you have spotted such an investment opportunity? Might you have predicted that tiny Compaq could become a *Fortune* 500 company, challenging powerhouse IBM in the process? If you don't think so, then you were not alone.

Today Compaq is a successful company with an outstanding reputation. Yet, back in 1983, many people viewed Compaq as just another computer company, competing with dozens of similar up-starts. In fact, *New Issues,* one of the leading newsletters to track IPOs, failed to include Compaq on its recommended buy list, although it did recommend a competitor, Kaypro. (Kaypro, incidentally, has since gone out of business.)

Clearly, our purpose isn't to criticize *New Issues,* which is cred-ited with recommending such stars as Autodesk and Stryker, both of which have increased in value by over 1,000%. (Peter Lynch, the renowned money manager from Fidelity, used the term *ten-bagger* to describe companies increasing in value by 10-fold, or 1,000%.)[1] Rather, we're suggesting that investors need a systematic method for distinguishing potential "winners" from "losers" and of differentiat-ing between two or more companies within the same industry, both of which may appear to be equally attractive investments. Our ap-proach does just this, as we will demonstrate shortly, when we apply our framework to Compaq and Kaypro.

Could our model have predicted the tremendous success of Compaq? The answer is yes! According to our framework, there were several factors indicating that Compaq would excel. Using our model, Compaq received one of our highest ratings and consequently, it was not too surprising that Compaq's stock increased by 500% in value since its IPO.

OUR SOURCE OF INFORMATION—READING THE PROSPECTUS

What information is available about these new issues? Where can an individual investor obtain this information? Fortunately, the vital information for making investment decisions on emerging growth ventures is to be found in a *prospectus*—a free, publicly avail-able report supplied by the underwriter who is selling the stock in the company. It can be obtained from the underwriter directly or from most stock brokers. Our research suggests that the information con-tained in a company's prospectus often provides important clues in predicting both successful and unsuccessful investments.

---

[1] Peter Lynch. *One Up On Wall Street.* Simon & Schuster, 1989.

INVESTING IN INITIAL PUBLIC OFFERINGS

Privately-held growth companies often go public for a number of reasons. These include:

* Increasing the company's financial base
* Increasing the liquidity of the owners
* Increasing the prestige of the company
* Increasing the company's ability to attract management
* Strengthening the company's position to make future acquisitions.

Typically, a company that goes public is relatively young with sales of $5 million to $50 million and is growing rapidly. However, there are many "atypical" IPOs, including:

* *Spin-offs or subsidiaries from well-established companies.* For example, Atlantic Richfield spun off its Lyondell Petrochemical subsidiary in a $1 billion IPO.
* *Deleveraging, following a leveraged buy-out (LBOs).* For example, Safeway Stores recently went public, after Kohlberg, Kravis & Roberts (KKR) took the company private.
* *Old-line, well-established, privately-held companies.* For example, Reader's Digest Association had been a private company for 67 years prior to its IPO.
* *Closed-end mutual funds.* For example, the New Germany Fund went public during 1990.

The main focus of our book is the *small, young, high-growth* company.

What Is a Prospectus?

Whenever a company plans to sell securities to the public it must register with the Securities and Exchange Commission (SEC) and supply a prospectus to both the Commission and any interested investors. The act of reading the prospectus can prove to be very valuable for an investor. The prospectus contains a detailed business plan, describing the company's history, future plans, competition, management, and directors, and its financial condition. It outlines how the company plans to use the proceeds from the offering and it

---

THE PROSPECTUS

A typical prospectus generally contains the following sections:

A. Prospectus Summary
B. Description of the Company
C. Risk Factors
D. Use of Proceeds
E. Dividend Policy
F. Capitalization
G. Dilution
H. Selected Consolidated Financial Data
I. Management Discussion and Analysis
J. Description of the Business (detailed)
K. Management and Directors
L. Certain Transactions
M. Principal and Selling Shareholders
N. Shares Eligible for Future Sale
O. Description of Capital Stock
P. Underwriters
Q. Legal Matters
R. Experts
S. Audited Financial Statements

highlights any important risks facing investors. Such information contained in the prospectus often influences a potential investor's decision on whether or not to invest.

Follow-Up to the Prospectus

The prospectus for a new issue is well known because it is a vital part of the IPO process. However, the investor should remember that subsequent to its IPO, a company traded publicly is required to file additional information at the SEC. Specifically, companies must file: 1. Form 10–Q (quarterly financial statements due 45 days after the end of a quarter); 2. Form 10–K (annual financial statements due 90 days after the year-end); 3. Form 8–K (notification of any important transaction, change of auditors, and so forth); and 4. various other filings, whenever important developments occur. The 10–Q and 10–K are similar to yet less detailed than the prospectus, and could, therefore, be used for analysis by investors. All documents are readily available from the investor relations department of any publicly traded company.

While much of our analysis and discussion in this book centers on the prospectus, it is important to remember that a prospectus is only a snapshot of a company at a single point in time, the period right before it issues stock to the public. To evaluate a company as time passes adequately and as new information about the company becomes available, you must continue to analyze new information. For example, in the prospectus for Cray Research at the time of its IPO, the auditor gave the company a "qualified" opinion, questioning Cray's ability to continue as a going concern, due to its early stage of development. Subsequent 10–Ks, however, revealed that the auditors gave the company a clean opinion. Thus, it is important to continue monitoring a company's progress by reading subsequent 10–Ks, 10–Qs, and other important filings.

COMPAQ: SEARCHING FOR *TURNONS* AND *TURNOFFS*

Let's now use Compaq's 1983 prospectus and identify what factors "turned us on" and what factors "turned us off" at the time of its IPO. The discussion on Compaq that follows is an example of how to use our framework.

THE 10–K

A 10–K usually contains the following sections:

- Audited Balance Sheet (past two years)
- Audited Statement of Income (past three years)
- Audited Statement of Cash Flow (past three years)
- Footnotes to the Financial Statement
- Management Discussion and Analysis
- Letter from the Auditor
- Liquidity Position and Capital Resources
- Litigation Pending
- Description of the Company's Business and History
- Directors and Executive Officers
- Related Party Transactions

Turnons—Signals of a Strong Investment

In examining Compaq's prospectus we noticed the following attractive features which we label "turnons:"

1. Expanding market and rapid revenue growth
2. Outstanding managers and directors
3. Solid balance sheet, strong earnings, and cash flow from operations
4. Fair financial arrangement for new investors

Expanding Market. Compaq's prospectus outlined the most recent sales revenue for the company. Since Compaq went public during its first full year of operation, its sales were presented for each quarter as follows:

PERIOD	SALES
Quarter ending March 31	$5 million
Quarter ending June 30	$18 million
Quarter ending Sept 30	$36 million

By any measure, Compaq's first year growth was remarkable, with nearly $60 million in sales during its first nine months of operation, and sales increasing dramatically from quarter to quarter. From its inception, Compaq was able to establish dealer networks with such important vendors as Businessland, Computerland, Sears Business Systems, and several other well known retailers. Establishing a strong dealer network is important for such early stage companies as Compaq. After all, it enables a company to have a strong sales force ready to sell its product. In essence, it demonstrates clearly that Compaq had a stable and reliable market for its product.

Outstanding Managers and Directors. Compaq assembled a strong management team, including former managers from Texas Instruments and IBM. In addition, Compaq had three outstanding outside directors, each of whom was an experienced venture capitalist: Ben Rosen (the company's chairman, who was also a director of Lotus Development), L.J. Sevin (founder of Mostek), and John Doerr (a partner in the respected venture capital firm, Kleiner Perkins Caufield & Byers). Venture capitalists, who are often considered among the most astute and successful investors, generally agree that a *solid management team* is the best predictor for the success of an emerging venture.

VENTURE CAPITALISTS GENERALLY AGREE THAT A SOLID MANAGEMENT TEAM IS THE BEST PREDICTOR FOR THE SUCCESS OF AN EMERGING VENTURE.

Solid Balance Sheet. Financially, Compaq was in fairly strong shape. It had nearly $17 million in working capital (excess of short-term assets over short-term debt) and had a manageable level of debt. Similar to most start-up companies, however, it still had cumulative net losses. Nonetheless, in the quarter immediately prior to its IPO (but still during its first year of operation), Compaq generated a respectable profit, unusual for a start-up computer company. Most of the capital raised by Compaq from this stock offering was targeted for expansion and for future growth. A portion of the funds were targeted for repayment of debt, which would strengthen Compaq's short term debt position. Overall, Compaq was in an attractive financial position for an early stage, high tech venture.

Fair Financial Arrangement. The fact that Compaq already had raised nearly $30 million in capital prior to its IPO from venture capitalists Sevin Rosen, Kleiner Perkins Caufield & Byers, Humboldt Trust, and L.F. Rothschild, as well as from others, should have excited potential investors. Furthermore, none of these investors (nor anyone else, for that matter) was selling its shares of Compaq at the time it went public. Thus, the sophisticated private investors, who had first-hand knowledge of Compaq and who had been monitoring its progress carefully, not only decided to invest in Compaq in the first place, but also decided to retain their ownership when it went public. We consider these factors as important turnons for potential investors.

Turnoffs—Signals of a Weak Investment

Of course, not everything about Compaq's initial public offering was attractive; Compaq could hardly be characterized as a "can't miss" opportunity for new public investors. Remember, Compaq was a one-year old company in a highly competitive industry, initially valued at nearly one-half billion dollars. In addition, new investors would be paying 12 times the price paid by the existing shareholders.

Rarely do we find an investment opportunity with no *turnoffs*. In the case of Compaq, the *turnons* significantly outnumbered and outweighed the *turnoffs*. Could we have predicted a 5-fold increase in Compaq's stock price over the subsequent six years? Probably not. However, there were so many significant *turnons* associated with Compaq, that it was reasonable to predict that the stock *could have* performed exceedingly well, especially in the 1983 bull market for technology companies.

COMPARING COMPAQ TO KAYPRO

During the late 1970s and early 1980s, many computer manufacturers such as Apple, Compaq, Kaypro, Osborne, Columbia Data Products, and Vector Graphic were in their infancy. Yet, over subsequent years some have prospered while others have faltered.

For example, since its IPO seven years ago, Compaq has become a notable success while Kaypro has became a major disappointment. Back in 1983, could investors have differentiated these two companies, both of whom were making the same product for the same market? Would an investor who read the prospectus of each company have become excited about Compaq and concerned about Kaypro? Were there any clues which could have alerted us to the probable winners and losers? To answer these questions, we decided to compare the prospectuses of Compaq to Kaypro carefully, both early-stage computer manufacturers that went public about the same time.

By applying our framework, we found many important differences between these two companies which suggested that investors should clearly invest in Compaq and pass up Kaypro. Here are some of the significant concerns that we found in reading Kaypro's prospectus:

1. *Past Performance:* Unlike Compaq, which was a new, high-growth company (with $60 million in revenue during its first 9 months), Kaypro was a 30-year old, low-growth business, founded under the name Non-Linear Systems, Inc., and generating only $5 million in sales in the year prior to going public. From its inception until 1981, Kaypro was involved exclusively in developing, manufacturing, and selling a line of sophisticated electronic instruments, many for aerospace and defense applications. It began selling microcomputer systems in June 1982 only, just 14 months prior to going public.

2. *Product:* Kaypro took some significant risks by designing its computers using the CP/M operating system (which is not IBM compatible), as compared to Compaq, which used the DOS operating system (IBM compatible).

3. *Strategy:* Unlike Compaq, whose niche strategy was to capture the high price/high margin segment of the market, Kaypro tried

to attract the highly competitive, low price/low margin segment of the market.

4. *Suppliers/Dealers:* Kaypro was beginning to experience difficulty in obtaining an adequate supply of disk drives for its products, resulting in delays in shipping computers to its customers. Also, Kaypro had been sued by a former dealer who sought damages.

5. *Management:* This is perhaps the most important element. Unlike Compaq, which had a diverse executive team, with management experience at such high growth companies as IBM and Texas Instruments, Kaypro was essentially a family run business. Furthermore, Kaypro lacked the type of sophisticated outside directors who were so important to Compaq's early (and sustained) success. Kaypro's officers and directors, most of whom were family members, included:

   a. Andrew Kay—Chairman and CEO
   b. David Kay—Vice-President Marketing
   c. Allan Kay—Vice-President Administration
   d. Mary Kay (not the cosmetics entrepreneur)—Secretary and Director

Our concern was that family members, rather than the most talented managers, were in these responsible corporate positions at Kaypro. And from our personal experiences, we (the Schilit brothers) have learned that working closely with siblings or other family members at times can be both stressful and, in a word, dysfunctional. At Kaypro, which had four members of its family in executive positions, conflict and dissension were almost inevitable.

As noted in a recent article in *Forbes* magazine describing the demise of Kaypro, the author speculated that a major problem at Kaypro was nepotism; i.e., "too many Kays and not enough pros."[2] Sure enough, family squabbles frequently created problems at Kaypro. Marketing executive David Kay was often at odds with his dad, CEO Andrew. According to Andrew, "we had a communication problem."

---

[2] Julie Pitta. "We Had a Communication Problem." *Forbes*, May 28, 1990, pp. 344ff.

*A MAJOR PROBLEM AT KAYPRO WAS NEPO-
TISM; i.e., "TOO MANY KAYS AND NOT ENOUGH
PROS."*

6. *Related Transactions:* At Kaypro, there were a series of related
   party transactions involving the Kay family; not the kind of
   arrangements which would please outside investors. Among
   the more problematic of these related party transactions were
   the following:
   a. The company leased its land, building, and equipment from
      Andrew Kay
   b. The company loaned Andrew Kay $250,000, apparently for
      personal reasons
   c. Kaypro made several additional loans of almost $500,000 to
      Andrew Kay
   d. The company paid $16,000 for advertising to a company
      owned by David Kay

   Such transactions weakened the overall credibility of the company.
7. *Financials:* The financial statements of Kaypro clearly showed a
   struggling company with recurring losses from operations.
   Here are examples of some of its financial problems:
   a. Although Kaypro had had a substantial increase in recent
      sales, it had posted *losses* from operations.
   b. Kaypro's inventory seemed to be growing too quickly, rais-
      ing the possibility that if sales were to drop, Kaypro would
      have to unload its inventory at discounted prices. This was
      a potentially damaging situation for a high tech company,
      faced with the risk of product obsolescence.
   c. Kaypro's current liabilities had been growing rapidly, re-
      sulting in a weakened liquidity position.

Thus, it was not surprising that over the years, Compaq and
Kaypro moved in opposite directions. Compaq grew rapidly and
today it generates over $3 billion in revenues and has a market

valuation of approximately $5 billion. Kaypro, which at one time was valued at almost $400 million, is now bankrupt and its stock is no longer traded on a national exchange.

ONE MORE EXAMPLE: COMPARING GENENTECH TO GENEX

We have also examined and compared two genetic engineering start-ups of the early 1980s—Genentech, of San Francisco, and Genex, of Washington, D.C. In comparing these companies we have found clear similarities and profound differences:

1. Both were in the start-up phase, generating less than $4 million in revenues from contract services, with none of the revenues from sales of products.

2. Both companies relied on an impressive group of scientists with substantial experience in the emerging field of genetic engineering.

3. Genentech had a CEO with a strong management background and a chairperson (Thomas Perkins, of the venture capital firm Kleiner Perkins Caufield & Byers) who also was chairperson of the successful Tandem Computer Company. Genex, on the other hand, had a CEO with experience mainly as a scientist, although he had served as the former CEO and chairperson of a company which later declared bankruptcy.

4. Genentech engaged in no questionable related party transactions and provided no interest-free loans to employees. Genex, on the the other hand, had a separate consulting relationship with its chairperson; it also provided interest-free loans to its employees.

5. The financial condition of Genentech was stronger than that of Genex substantially. Genentech had a substantial amount of cash, while Genex was cash poor.

Over the years since Genentech and Genex went public, there has been a stark difference in their relative performances, as measured by their sales and market values. While Genentech's sales have grown steadily to over $300 million, Genex's sales peaked at $26 million in 1984, and later plummeted to $1.6 million by 1987. In terms of market value, Genentech's stock had become a *ten-bagger* by 1987, while Genex's stock has lost almost all its value.

HOW DO WE DEFINE SUCCESSFUL COMPANIES?

One Day Climbs

At times, an investor can do exceedingly well by buying a new issue at its opening price and, perhaps, cashing out (selling his or her stock) immediately afterwards if there is an increase in the stock price. For example, on October 4, 1980, Genentech went public at $35 a share. It traded as high as $89 on that day, before closing at $71. Home Shopping Network (HSN) had a similar, although somewhat less remarkable, run-up on the day of its IPO. However, it must be emphasized that:

1. A limited number of shares are allocated to each brokerage company. Thus, only a select group of investors will be able to go along on the "joy ride" from the *opening bell*. How do you get to be one of those privileged investors? It's earned by developing a track record with brokers by buying *all* new issues. That means you have to take the good ones as well as the junk.

2. The reason that these stocks often increased in value on their first day of trading, in most cases, was not due to their fundamentals, but rather, due to the hype surrounding them. The reason that such stocks either continue to appreciate or come crashing down, however, is usually due to fundamentals. Genentech's further appreciation over the long term was due to its innovative products, its quality management, and its strong financial position. On the other hand, there were weak fundamentals associated with HSN, thereby resulting in an eventual drastic decline in its stock price.

THAT THESE STOCKS INCREASED IN VALUE ON THEIR FIRST DAY OF TRADING WAS NOT DUE TO THEIR FUNDAMENTALS, BUT RATHER, DUE TO THE HYPE SURROUNDING THEM.

3. These huge one-day advances *rarely* occur; we may see them once every few years. So, although your broker might be pressuring you to buy a company that will be "the next Genentech," you might find that it turns out to be "the next Genex." If it's a quality company, there will be time to buy the company an hour, a day, a week, a month, or a year after it goes public, and *still* make phenomenal returns. An investor who bought shares in The Gap in 1983 (several years after it went public) still could have realized a 14-fold increase in value by 1989.

> *IF IT'S A QUALITY COMPANY, THERE WILL BE TIME TO BUY THE COMPANY AN HOUR, A DAY, A WEEK, A MONTH, OR A YEAR AFTER IT GOES PUBLIC, AND STILL MAKE PHENOMENAL RETURNS.*

4. The first day's stock price rise will be insignificant, relative to its long term performance, provided that it's a quality company. Consider investors who purchased Genentech at $71 per share a day after it went public. Even though they lost out on the massive initial run-up in the company's stock, they still would have made a 500% return on their investment had they held onto their stock for the next seven years.

Quality Companies Appreciate Over the Long Term

"Success" (as related to investments) is difficult to define, particularly with speculative investments that often fluctuate in price from month to month, or even from day to day significantly. If the stock market is doing well, IPOs often do fairly well. In fact, on average, when the overall stock market is performing well, IPOs are likely to appreciate 5–10% during the first few days of trading, fueled largely by hype or publicity. As we pointed out earlier, our approach ignores the initial short term price spurt of a company. Instead, we focus on the long term outlook for a company. In other words, we try to gauge whether the IPO is a *quality* company over the long term, based on our analysis of certain key factors (which are examined in the following chapters.)

Our definition of success is based on *long term investment value.* This means that although it is generally most attractive to purchase stock in a promising young company *on the day* of its IPO, it will, in most situations, *still* be an attractive value several months later, if it was a good value when it first went public. No doubt, it will be more costly. But, if it's a quality company, it will still have substantial market appreciation several years after going public. For example, an investor who purchased Wal-Mart in 1980 at a price-adjusted $0.88 per share (a decade *after* it first went public) still could have realized a 50–fold increase by 1989.

OUR DEFINITION OF SUCCESS IS BASED ON **LONG TERM INVESTMENT VALUE....** *IF IT'S A QUALITY COMPANY, IT WILL STILL HAVE SUBSTANTIAL APPRECIATION SEVERAL YEARS AFTER GOING PUBLIC.*

One thing is quite evident when it comes to selecting stocks: Over the long term, quality, rather than hype or temporary market conditions, prevails. As Peter Lynch, one of the greatest stock-pickers of recent times, recently noted in his best selling book, *One Up On Wall Street,*

> In the end, superior companies will succeed and mediocre companies will fail, and investors in each will be rewarded accordingly.[3]

Consequently, we disregard day-to-day fluctuations. We measure success largely by a consistent appreciation in the stock price *over a number of years.* Moreover, we measure success *relative to the overall stock market.* Many IPOs perform quite well during a dramatic short term rise in the overall stock market. However, it takes a high quality

---

[3] Lynch, op. cit.

company—such as Compaq, Apple, or Microsoft—to consistently outperform the market over a long time horizon.

> *OVER THE LONG TERM, QUALITY, RATHER THAN HYPE OR TEMPORARY MARKET CONDITIONS, PREVAILS.... WE MEASURE SUCCESS LARGELY BY A CONSISTENT APPRECIATION IN THE STOCK PRICE OVER A NUMBER OF YEARS. MOREOVER, WE MEASURE SUCCESS RELATIVE TO THE OVERALL STOCK MARKET.*

One more issue of concern regarding success and failure: Certainly, Compaq's eight-fold increase in stock value since it went public in 1983, coupled with its twenty-five-fold increase in sales and its substantial increase in profits, would be considered a success story. Conversely, Kaypro, a company which went public in 1983, and subsequently went bankrupt, would be labeled a failure. However, it is more difficult to classify a company like Home Shopping Network (HSN), which went public at $18 per share in 1986, then increased in value to $38, before plummeting to $4. Despite its early appreciation in stock price, we would classify HSN as a "failure" since it has not proven to be an attractive *long term* investment. A much more extreme example of a "loser" is Silk Greenhouse, which went public at $11 per share, then doubled in value, before eventually losing almost all of its market value

Other Successes and Failures

There are numerous other success stories—for example, Microsoft, Federal Express, Apple Computer, Home Depot—each of which rewarded investors with hefty returns. Similarly, there are many *more* horror stories of business failures including such companies as ZZZZ Best, Crazy Eddie, and Vector Graphic. There are also numerous recent IPOs—such as Home Shopping Network and Silk Greenhouse—which have titillated investors with their rapid ascent, only to later disappoint them with their sudden and deep decline. Our research has shown that in *most* cases, the eventual outcome was *predictable*, based on information that was available to the investor readily. This information was found in the prospectuses of those companies and, in some cases, in the subsequent 10–Ks, 10–Qs, and other reports filed with the SEC.

Throughout this book we recount the many interesting stories of some of the most famous and infamous IPOs of the past two decades, and we demonstrate how our framework can help you to predict the long-term success or failure of specific companies.

OUR APPROACH—WATCH OUT FOR THOSE MESSY BUFFALO CHIPS

Looking for *Red Flags*

There are substantial risks for those who invest in young emerging growth companies. Stock-pickers and brokers like to talk about the "home runs" they have hit. But what about their losers? Like the home run hitters in baseball or the long ball drivers in golf, we question the value of hitting just a few home runs if the batter usually strikes out while "swinging for the fences;" or similarly, we question the value of driving a golf ball 300 yards, if the golfer's next shot is in a water hazard.

Our approach is one that avoids swinging wildly for home runs *all the time*; sometimes, it's more important to avoid a strikeout. Therefore, we try to keep our risk exposure as low as possible. We try to avoid the strikeouts and avoid the losers; this we feel is as important as always trying for winners. Our approach is to look for *red flags* and thus be ready to avoid certain investments. Being alert to red flags might mean that you would want to avoid buying a stock in the first place or to sell a stock that you already own.

Using our approach, we have found such red flags as the following in reading some prospectuses: Electronics retailer Crazy Eddie disclosed in its prospectus that: 1. it funded a medical school in the Caribbean; 2. it invested in oil and gas limited partnerships; and 3. it made interest free loans to its chairperson and family. Shortly after its public offering, the company filed for bankruptcy. Likewise, Los Angeles based carpet cleaning company ZZZZ Best's prospectus was filled with red flags. The prospectus disclosed that it was being sued by someone who had borrowed money from the company at a rate that exceeded the maximum permitted by law. Shortly after going public, ZZZZ Best filed for bankruptcy and its founder, Barry Minkow, was sentenced to 25 years in prison for securities fraud and other violations.

Avoiding Mistakes

IPOs are risky investments. While some—such as Compaq, Microsoft, Apple and Federal Express—have become superstars, others such as ZZZZ Best, DeLaurentiis Entertainment, Vector Graphic, and Pizza Time Theatre have become footnotes in history. The well-respected IPO newsletter, *New Issues*, has been wrong *more than half the time* in predicting successful emerging growth companies. A review of the newletter's picks reveals that approximately 60% of its recommendations (and, recently, *two-thirds* of its current portfolio) have lost money, including many which have lost *most*, or even *all*, of their value.

One of our goals is to offer you an approach that helps you to be successful a lot more than 40% of the time. As we've said earlier, IPOs should *not* be viewed as a "crap shoot" at a casino. Rather, by using a systematic model based on carefully researched historical information, investing in emerging growth companies could prove to be quite lucrative. Obviously, we can't guarantee that you will always find investments that increase by 10-fold (i.e., the ten baggers.) In reality, very few investments perform at that level. Only 2–3% of the recommendations in *New Issues* have increased by that amount; by contrast, dozens have lost more than 80% of their value. Nonetheless, we have found that by investing in companies that have several turnons and relatively few turnoffs, you can improve your investment performance considerably.

We are not stock-pickers. As we said earlier, this task is left to you and your advisors. Rather, we offer you a *framework* that helps discriminate the likely "superstars" from the "superduds." After you become familiar with our model, all that remains is for you to read the prospectuses to begin to separate the *red chips* from the *buffalo chips*.

just this reason. Ironically, HSN has ironed out many of its earlier problems and is considered a much stronger company today than it was at the time of its IPO.

Why do some early stage ventures perform remarkably well while others—often in the same industry during the same time period (for example Compaq vs. Kaypro or Genentech vs. Genex)—fail? Is there a way to predict whether an emerging growth business will be a smashing success or a dismal failure? Is there a way for investors to increase the likelihood of investing in "winners" (red chips) and decrease the likelihood of investing in "losers" (buffalo chips)? These are the central questions that we address.

As part of our long term study, we have found that a careful analysis of early stage ventures, even before they go public, often provides vital information which helps us predict their after-market stock performance. As we suggested earlier, such information is publicly available and is found in the prospectus, which can be obtained from a participating underwriter of a new issue or from a stock broker.

We have examined over one hundred prospectuses of companies and have classified these companies as either "winners" or "losers," based on their subsequent stock market performance.

The "Winners"[1]

A sampling of the best performing recent IPOs over the long term, along with graphs to illustrate their post-IPO performance, is as follows:

---

[1] *Current* valuations for the "winners" and "losers" are based on their December 31, 1990 stock price.

APPLE COMPUTER: Apple designs, develops, produces, and markets personal computer systems. It was founded in 1977 by entrepreneurs Steven P. Jobs and Stephen G. Wozniak and it went public in December 1980 in a $100 million offering. At the time of its IPO, the company had sales of $100 million and was valued at approximately $1 billion. Today, Apple generates sales of $6 billion and is valued at around $5 billion.

APPLE COMPUTER CORPORATION
Stock Price Movement 1980-1990

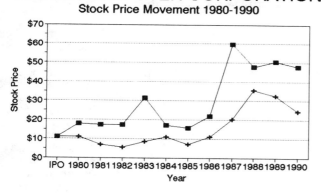

Apple Computer		
	Price	
Year	High	Low
IPO	$11.00	$11.00
1980	$18.00	$11.00
1981	$17.30	$6.80
1982	$17.40	$5.40
1983	$31.60	$8.60
1984	$17.20	$10.90
1985	$15.60	$7.10
1986	$21.90	$10.90
1987	$59.80	$20.10
1988	$47.80	$35.50
1989	$50.40	$32.50
1990	$47.75	$24.25

ATLANTIC RESEARCH: Atlantic manufactures and develops solid propellant rocket motors and data communications test equipment, and performs electromagnetic engineering services. It was founded in 1949 and in 1967 was merged into The Susquehanna Corporation. In 1972, Susquehanna reorganized the company, preserving the name Atlantic Research. The company went public in 1979 in a $5 million offering. At that time the company had sales of $28 million and was valued at approximately $40 million. Atlantic Research, after appreciating in value considerably over the next few years, was acquired by the ORI Group, Inc. in 1987.

ATLANTIC RESEARCH CORP.
Stock Price Movement 1979-1987

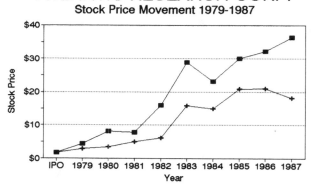

Atlantic Research Cor Price		
Year	High	Low
IPO	$1.77	$1.77
1979	$4.38	$2.88
1980	$8.13	$3.50
1981	$7.88	$5.00
1982	$16.00	$6.13
1983	$28.75	$15.88
1984	$23.13	$15.00
1985	$30.00	$20.88
1986	$32.25	$21.00
1987	$36.50	$18.25

■— High for the year   +— Low for the year

AUTODESK: Autodesk designs, develops, markets, and supports computer-aided design and drafting (CAD) software for use on leading desktop computers. It was founded in 1982 by entrepreneurs John Walker, Keith Marcelius, and Daniel Drake and it went public in 1985 in a $15 million offering. At that time the company had sales of under $10 million and was valued at approximately $68 million. Today, Autodesk generates sales of $200 million and is valued at over $1 billion.

AUTODESK INC.
Stock Price Movement 1985-1990

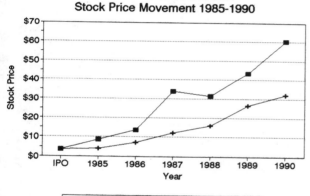

Year	Autodesk Price High	Low
IPO	$3.66	$3.66
1985	$8.50	$4.00
1986	$13.40	$7.10
1987	$34.00	$12.00
1988	$31.30	$16.00
1989	$43.50	$26.50
1990	$60.25	$32.00

■ High for the year + Low for the year

CIRCUS CIRCUS: Circus Circus owns and operates the Circus Circus casino-hotels in the area commonly known as the "Strip" in Las Vegas, Nevada, and in Reno, Nevada. It began operations in 1974 and went public in 1983. At that time the company had annualized sales in excess of $200 million and was valued at approximately $280 million. Today, Circus Circus generates sales in excess of $1/2 billion and is valued at over $1 billion.

CIRCUS CIRCUS ENTERPRISES
Stock Price Movement 1983-1990

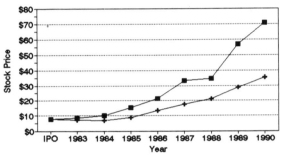

Circus Circus Enterprises Inc.

Year	Price High	Low
IPO	$7.50	$7.50
1983	$8.50	$7.20
1984	$9.90	$6.80
1985	$15.30	$8.70
1986	$21.30	$13.40
1987	$33.50	$17.50
1988	$34.80	$20.90
1989	$57.00	$28.80
1990	$70.88	$35.75

—■— High for the year   —+— Low for the year

COMPAQ COMPUTER: Compaq designs, develops, manufactures, and markets personal computers for business and professional use. It began operations in February 1982, shipped its first product in January 1983, and went public in December 1983. At that time the company had annualized sales in excess of $75 million and was valued at approximately $450 million. Today, Compaq generates sales of $3 billion and is valued at around $5 billion.

COMPAQ COMPUTER CORP.
Stock Price Movement 1983-1990

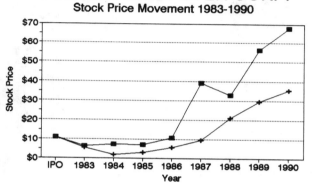

Compaq Computer Price

Year	High	Low
IPO	$11.00	$11.00
1983	$6.30	$5.50
1984	$7.30	$1.80
1985	$7.10	$3.10
1986	$10.80	$5.80
1987	$39.30	$9.60
1988	$32.90	$21.00
1989	$56.30	$29.60
1990	$67.88	$35.50

— High for the year   —+— Low for the year

COSTCO WAREHOUSE: Costco operates a chain of wholesale membership warehouses that sell national brand merchandise at low prices to businesses, primarily for commercial use or resale. It opened its first warehouse in Seattle in September 1983 and went public in November 1985. At that time the company had annualized sales approximating $370 million and was valued at $200 million. Today, Costco generates sales of nearly $4 billion and is valued at around $2 billion.

COSTCO WHOLESALE CORP.
Stock Price Movement 1985-1990

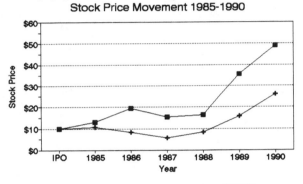

Costco Wholesale Corp.

Year	Price High	Low
IPO	$10.00	$10.00
1985	$13.10	$10.60
1986	$19.50	$8.50
1987	$15.30	$5.60
1988	$16.30	$8.40
1989	$35.60	$15.80
1990	$49.00	$26.00

FEDERAL EXPRESS: Federal Express provides door-to-door delivery of packages throughout the U.S. and abroad, primarily on an overnight basis. The company operates its own integrated air-ground transportation system designed exclusively for the high priority shipment of small packages. Federal Express was founded in 1971 by Frederick W. Smith and went public in 1978. At that time, the company had annualized sales in excess of $150 million and was valued at approximately $80 million. Today, Federal Express generates sales of more than $6 billion and is valued at around $2 billion.

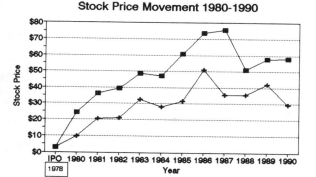

FEDERAL EXPRESS CORP.
Stock Price Movement 1980-1990

Federal Express Corp.

Year	Price High	Low
IPO	$3.00	$3.00
1980	$24.40	$9.70
1981	$36.10	$20.30
1982	$39.40	$20.80
1983	$48.50	$32.60
1984	$47.00	$27.80
1985	$61.00	$31.40
1986	$73.80	$51.00
1987	$75.50	$35.30
1988	$51.00	$35.40
1989	$57.90	$42.10
1990	$58.00	$29.50

HOME DEPOT: Home Depot operates retail "warehouse" stores that sell a wide assortment of building materials and home improvement products. Sales, which are primarily cash-and-carry, are concentrated in the do-it-yourself and home remodeling markets. It was incorporated in 1978 by Bernard Marcus and Arthur M. Blank and went public in 1981. At that time the company had annualized sales in excess of $37 million and was valued at approximately $30 million. Today, Home Depot generates sales of $3 billion and is valued at over $4 billion.

HOME DEPOT INC.
Stock Price Movement 1981-1990

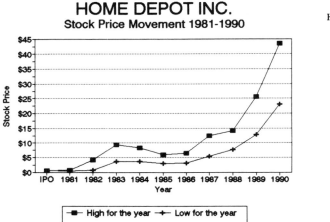

Home Depot Inc.

Year	Price High	Low
IPO	$0.59	$0.59
1981	$0.80	$0.50
1982	$4.30	$0.70
1983	$9.40	$3.60
1984	$8.30	$3.60
1985	$6.00	$3.10
1986	$6.40	$3.20
1987	$12.50	$5.30
1988	$14.20	$7.70
1989	$25.60	$12.80
1990	$43.50	$23.00

KING WORLD PRODUCTIONS: King World has been engaged since 1964 in the distribution or syndication of television programs to television stations throughout the U.S. The company distributes various television series and news insert programs produced independently, including Wheel of Fortune, Jeopardy and The Oprah Winfrey Show. At the time King World went public in 1984 it had annualized sales of nearly $30 million and was valued at approximately $50 million. Today, King World generates sales of $1/2 billion and is valued at around $1 billion.

KING WORLD PRODUCTIONS INC.
Stock Price Movement 1984-1990

King World Productions Inc.

		Price
Year	High	Low
IPO	$1.11	$1.11
1984	$1.70	$1.10
1985	$6.80	$1.40
1986	$12.80	$6.80
1987	$22.20	$8.70
1988	$17.80	$10.60
1989	$27.10	$15.30
1990	$30.00	$18.13

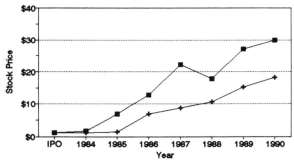

LIZ CLAIBORNE: Liz Claiborne designs, contracts for the manufacture of, and markets an extensive range of clothing under the LIZ CLAIBORNE and LIZ trademarks. Since the founding of the company in 1976, it has concentrated on identifying and furnishing the wardrobe requirements of the business and professional woman. At the time the company went public it had annualized sales in excess of $100 million and was valued at the level of its annualized sales. Today, Liz Claiborne generates sales of $2 billion and is valued at more than $2 billion.

LIZ CLAIBORNE INC.
Stock Price Movement 1981-1990

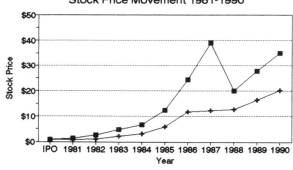

Liz Claiborne Inc.

Year	Price High	Low
IPO	$0.79	$0.79
1981	$1.30	$0.80
1982	$2.60	$1.00
1983	$4.70	$2.00
1984	$6.60	$3.10
1985	$12.40	$5.90
1986	$24.30	$11.90
1987	$39.10	$12.30
1988	$20.00	$12.80
1989	$27.80	$16.50
1990	$35.00	$20.25

LOTUS DEVELOPMENT: Lotus designs, produces, and markets its own application software packages for use with personal computers for business and professional applications. The company's initial product, 1–2–3, offers an integrated solution to a variety of common business and productivity problems by combining spreadsheet, database, and graphing capabilities into a single program. It began operations in April 1982, shipped its first product in January 1983, and went public in October 1983. At that time, the company had annualized sales in excess of $25 million and was valued at approximately $275 million. Today, Lotus generates sales of more than $1/2 billion and is valued at nearly $1 billion.

LOTUS DEVELOPMENT CORP.
Stock Price Movement 1983-1990

Lotus Development Corp.

Year	Price High	Low
IPO	$5.00	$5.00
1983	$10.30	$6.00
1984	$13.30	$5.10
1985	$11.30	$5.10
1986	$19.30	$6.70
1987	$39.80	$16.30
1988	$34.30	$14.80
1989	$33.50	$18.00
1990	$39.25	$12.50

—■— High for the year   —+— Low for the year

MICROSOFT: Microsoft designs, develops, markets, and supports a product line of systems and applications microcomputer software for business and professional use. The company offers application software in the following categories: word processing, spreadsheet, file management, graphics, communications, and project management. It began operations as a partnership in 1975 and was incorporated in 1981. At the time it went public in 1986, the company had annualized sales in excess of $170 million and was valued at approximately $1/2 billion. Today, Microsoft generates sales of more than $1 billion and is valued at approximately $9 billion.

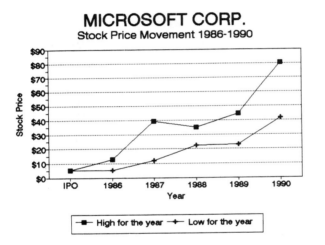

MICROSOFT CORP.
Stock Price Movement 1986-1990

Microsoft Corp.

Year	High	Low
IPO	$5.25	$5.25
1986	$12.80	$5.30
1987	$39.60	$11.90
1988	$35.30	$22.60
1989	$44.60	$22.90
1990	$80.75	$42.00

High for the year ― Low for the year

SBARRO: Sbarro develops and operates a national chain of family-style Italian restaurants under the Sbarro name. The Sbarro family has been engaged in the food service and restaurant business for approximately 30 years. At the time it went public in 1985 it had annualized sales in excess of $20 million and was valued at approximately $40 million. Today, Sbarro generates sales of nearly $200 million and is valued at around $1/2 billion.

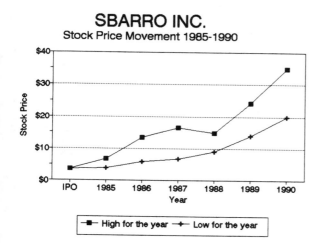

SBARRO INC.
Stock Price Movement 1985-1990

Sbarro Inc.

Year	Price High	Low
IPO	$3.45	$3.45
1985	$6.75	$3.75
1986	$13.38	$5.88
1987	$16.50	$6.75
1988	$14.88	$9.00
1989	$24.25	$13.88
1990	$34.88	$19.88

The "Losers"

Among the companies we have classified as "losers," that have either failed altogether or have experienced significant long-term declines in their stock prices, despite some earlier gains, are:

COLUMBIA DATA PRODUCTS: Columbia Data Products designed, developed, manufactured, and marketed personal computers for business and professional users. It began operations in February 1982, shipped its first product in January 1983, and went public in December 1983. At that time, the company had annualized sales in excess of $75 million and was valued at approximately $450 million. Shortly thereafter, it filed for bankruptcy.

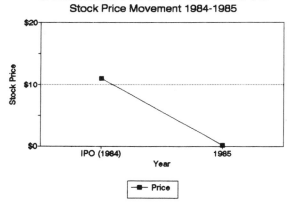

COLUMBIA DATA PRODUCTS
Stock Price Movement 1984-1985

Columbia Data Products	
	Price
Year	High
IPO (198	$11.00
1985	$0.13

GENEX: Genex applies recombinant DNA technology to the development of commercial products and processes. It concentrates its efforts on the application of genetic and biochemical engineering to the fields of specialty chemicals, food processing, feed additives, animal health care, and waste treatment. It began operations in 1977 and went public in 1982. At that time, the company had annualized sales in excess of $5 million and was valued at approximately $104 million. Today, Genex is valued at around $2 million.

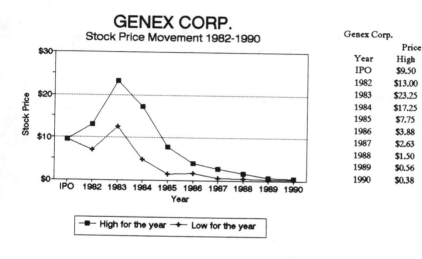

GENEX CORP.
Stock Price Movement 1982-1990

Genex Corp.

Year	Price High	Low
IPO	$9.50	$9.50
1982	$13.00	$7.00
1983	$23.25	$12.50
1984	$17.25	$4.75
1985	$7.75	$1.38
1986	$3.88	$1.50
1987	$2.63	$0.50
1988	$1.50	$0.38
1989	$0.56	$0.25
1990	$0.38	$0.25

HOME SHOPPING NETWORK: Home Shopping Network is a specialty retailer that markets a variety of consumer products by means of live, customer-interactive, televised sales programs broadcast over its own networks. The company evolved from management's experience using broadcast media to sell consumer goods in the Tampa Bay area. From 1977 to 1982, a business operated by Roy M. Speer and Lowell W. Paxson, the founders of Home Shopping Network (HSN), sold consumer goods over the radio. HSN began operations in 1982 and went public in 1986. At that time, the company had annual sales in excess of $125 million and was valued at approximately $250 million. Today, Home Shopping Network generates sales of approximately $1 billion and is valued at less than $1/2 billion.

HOME SHOPPING NETWORK INC.
Stock Price Movement 1986-1990

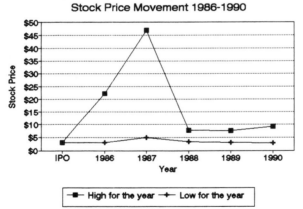

Home Shopping Network Inc.

	Price	
Year	High	Low
IPO	$3.00	$3.00
1986	$22.25	$3.00
1987	$47.00	$5.00
1988	$7.75	$3.38
1989	$7.63	$3.00
1990	$9.25	$2.88

KAYPRO: Kaypro develops, manufactures, and markets portable computers for business and personal users. From its incorporation in 1953 until it began developing microcomputers in 1981, Kaypro was engaged exclusively in developing, manufacturing, and selling sophisticated, electronic instruments used primarily in aerospace, defense, and industrial applications. At the time it went public, Kaypro had annualized sales in excess of $80 million and was valued at approximately $360 million. Shortly thereafter, Kaypro filed for bankruptcy.

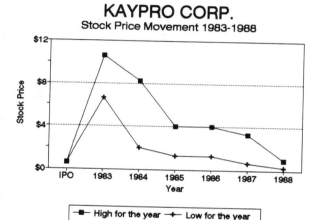

KAYPRO CORP.
Stock Price Movement 1983-1988

Kaypro Corp.

Year	Price High	Low
IPO	$0.59	$0.59
1983	$10.63	$6.63
1984	$8.25	$2.00
1985	$4.00	$1.25
1986	$4.00	$1.25
1987	$3.25	$0.63
1988	$0.88	$0.25

MAXICARE: Maxicare owns and operates a system of health maintenance organizations (HMOs). It arranges for comprehensive health care services to a population enrolled voluntarily for a predetermined, prepaid fee. It began operation in 1973 and by the time it went public in August 1983, it had annualized sales of $200 million and was valued at approximately $1/4 billion. Maxicare filed for bankruptcy and is no longer traded.

MAXICARE HEALTH PLANS INC.
Stock Price Movement 1983-1988

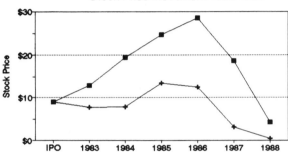

— High for the year —+— Low for the year

Maxicare Health Plans Inc.

	Price	
Year	High	Low
IPO	$9.00	$9.00
1983	$12.88	$7.75
1984	$19.38	$7.88
1985	$24.75	$13.50
1986	$28.50	$12.50
1987	$18.63	$3.13
1988	$4.25	$0.50

SILK GREENHOUSE: Silk Greenhouse operates warehouse-style stores that offer customers a broad selection of high quality artificial flowers, plants, and trees, as well as related decorating accessories, at competitively low prices. The company was founded in 1986 and is based in Tampa, Florida. At the time it went public in May 1988 the company had annualized sales in excess of $20 million and was valued at approximately $50 million. Silk Greenhouse, which filed for bankruptcy in 1990, is now valued at just $1 million.

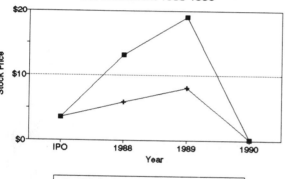

SILK GREENHOUSE
Stock Price Movement 1988-1990

Silk Greenhouse

Year	Price High	Low
IPO	$3.45	$3.45
1988	$13.13	$5.88
1989	$19.00	$8.00
1990	$0.13	$0.13

TELEVIDEO: Televideo designs, develops, manufactures, and markets video display terminals for the non-IBM market, personal computers, and multiuser microcomputer systems employing intelligent workstations. It began operations in 1976, shipped its first microcomputer in August 1981, and went public in March 1983. At that time, the company had annualized sales in excess of $100 million and was valued at approximately $3/4 billion. Today, Televideo, which is now generating only $50 million in revenues, is valued at only $11 million.

TELEVIDEO SYSTEMS INC.
Stock Price Movement 1983-1990

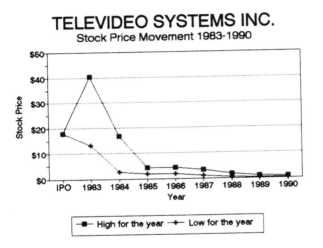

TeleVideo Systems Inc.

Year	Price High	Low
IPO	$18.00	$18.00
1983	$40.50	$13.25
1984	$16.75	$2.50
1985	$4.25	$1.75
1986	$4.13	$1.75
1987	$3.25	$1.00
1988	$1.63	$0.31
1989	$0.75	$0.19
1990	$0.63	$0.16

—■— High for the year   —+— Low for the year

TIE COMMUNICATIONS: TIE Communications designs and markets small and medium size multifeatured key telephone systems for business and residential use. It began operations in 1971 and went public in 1979. At that time, the company had annualized sales in excess of $30 million and was valued at approximately $13 million. After a significant run-up in the value of its stock, TIE is now valued at only $10 million.

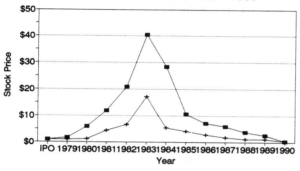

TIE Communications
Stock Price Movement 1979-1990

Tie Communications

Year	Price High	Low
IPO	$0.92	$0.92
1979	1.625	0.875
1980	$5.88	$1.13
1981	$11.88	$4.38
1982	$20.88	$6.63
1983	$40.38	$17.00
1984	$28.38	$5.50
1985	$10.63	$4.13
1986	$7.13	$2.75
1987	$5.88	$1.75
1988	$3.75	$1.13
1989	$2.50	$1.13
1990	$0.31	$0.31

   VECTOR GRAPHIC: Vector Graphic designed, developed, produced, and marketed a family of microcomputer systems with accompanying software for use by small businesses primarily in a wide
variety of data and word processing applications. It began operations
in 1976 and went public in 1981. At that time the company had
annualized sales in excess of $25 million and was valued at approxi-
mately $73 million. Vector Graphic, which declared bankruptcy
shortly after its IPO, is no longer traded.

VECTOR GRAPHIC INC.
Stock Price Movement 1981-1984

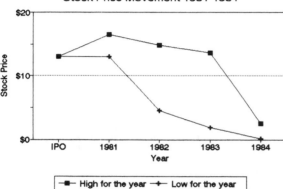

Vector Graphic Inc.

Year	Price High	Low
IPO	$13.00	$13.00
1981	$16.50	$13.00
1982	$14.88	$4.50
1983	$13.63	$1.88
1984	$2.50	$0.13

WORLDS OF WONDER: Worlds of Wonder designs, develops, markets, and distributes toy products. It was incorporated in March 1985, shipped its first product in August 1985, and went public in June 1986. At that time the company had annualized sales of nearly $100 million and was valued at approximately $400 million. Worlds of Wonder's success was short lived, and the company filed for bankruptcy within a year after its IPO.

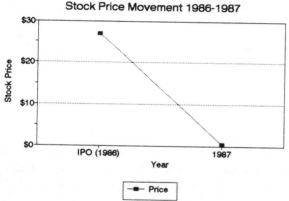

WORLDS OF WONDER
Stock Price Movement 1986-1987

Worlds of Wonder

Year	Price High
IPO (1986)	$27.00
1987	$0.50

ZZZZ BEST: ZZZZ Best provided professional residential and commercial carpet, upholstery, and drapery cleaning services throughout California. Its customers included homeowners and owners and operators of commercial establishments, such as hotels, restaurants, and office buildings. The company was a successor to the carpet cleaning business established in 1981 as a sole proprietorship by Barry J. Minkow, its CEO and sole shareholder. It was incorporated in 1985 as a wholly owned subsidiary of Morningstar Investments, Inc., an inactive Utah corporation. At the time it went public in December 1986, it had annualized sales in excess of $20 million and was valued at approximately $44 million. Within 8 months of its stock offering, the company's independent auditors learned of a massive fraud by ZZZZ Best, resulting in fictitious revenues and receivables. Today, CEO Minkow is serving a jail sentence and the company stock is worthless.

* * *

Searching for Peaks and Valleys

The previous charts demonstrate the cyclical nature of stocks. Rather than following a *straight* path upwards or downwards, stocks have a *general* movement upwards or downwards, indicative of the overall quality of the company.

There are also smaller up and down swings, which result from such factors as: short term earnings reports, overall economic and market conditions, the psychology of the market (i.e., greed, fear, and other emotions of the individual investor), and so forth. Thus, buying or selling a particular stock is not a once in a lifetime opportunity. There are usually many opportunities to do so. Of course, you can go searching for peaks and valleys and hope that you've bought at a low point and sold at a high point. Our feeling, however, is that, rather than looking solely at the short term fluctuations, which are exceedingly difficult to forecast, in order to spot a buying or selling opportunity, we concentrate on the overall trend of the particular stock. That means that you, as an investor, must ask yourself one basic question regarding a given stock: Is it a *quality* company that you would like to own for the forseeable future or is it a weak company destined for disaster?

ASK YOURSELF: IS IT A QUALITY COMPANY THAT YOU WOULD LIKE TO OWN OR IS IT A WEAK COMPANY DESTINED FOR DISASTER?

OUR SELECTION CRITERIA

What did it take to be included on our list of "winners" as compared to our list of "losers"? Our initial lists were based on a ranking of the performance of all companies that had gone public over the last 20 years. We identified the best performers and the worst performers—which should be quite clear from the above charts of their stock performance—and used that as our initial screening. We then condensed and revised our list to: 1. focus primarily on companies which had substantial name recognition; 2. select companies from several different industries; and 3. choose some "winners" and "losers" that have been competitors of one another—i.e., in the same industry during the same period of time.

DISTINGUISHING CHARACTERISTICS

Our goal was to find characteristics that differentiated the "winners" from the "losers". What did the "winners" have in common with each other? What did the "losers" have in common with each other?

The Predictors of Success and Failure: The *Turnons* and *Turnoffs*

Based on our research, we found that there were several common factors which we refer to as *predictive factors* that were excellent predictors of post-IPO stock market performance. We have grouped these predictive factors into the following four broad categories:

1. Product/Market
2. Management and Organization
3. Financial Position
4. Financial Arrangement

A description of the predictive factors—or *key indicators*—arranged by the above four broad categories, is presented in the following tables:

PREDICTIVE FACTOR: PRODUCT/MARKET		
PRODUCT/ MARKET FACTORS	TURNONS (Associated with the "winners")	TURNOFFS (Associated with the "losers")
1. Product/market focus	Clear	Disparate, unfocused
2. Competitive advantage	Distinct advantage in technology, quality, price, and so forth	Little or no advantages
3. Growth	Sustainable, high growth	Low growth, unsustainable
4. Operating history	Established company with a track record	Early stage venture
5. Linkages	Linkages with established companies	No such linkages

PREDICTIVE FACTOR: MANAGEMENT AND ORGANIZATION

MANAGEMENT AND ORGANIZATION FACTORS	TURNONS (Associated with the "winners")	TURNOFFS (Associated with the "losers")
1. Management team	Solid management team (and directors/ scientific advisors) with appropriate experience in this industry	Weak management team
2. Related transactions	Absence of questionable (e.g. related party) transactions	Existence of transactions
3. Litigation	No lawsuits against management or the company	Existence of lawsuits

PREDICTIVE FACTOR: FINANCIAL POSITION

FINANCIAL POSITION FACTORS	TURNONS (Associated with the "winners")	TURNOFFS (Associated with the "losers")
1. Earnings	Strong earnings and earnings growth	Weak earnings
2. Balance sheet and cash flows	Strong balance sheet and cash flows	Weak balance sheet and cash flows
3. Auditor's report	Audited financials with an unqualified opinion	Absence of audited financials or a qualified opinion

PREDICTIVE FACTOR: FINANCIAL ARRANGEMENT		
FINANCIAL ARRANGEMENT FACTORS	TURNONS (Associated with the "winners")	TURNOFFS (Associated with the "losers")
1. Use of proceeds	Targeted to fuel growth	To repay debt; for general use
2. Selling shareholders	Few shareholders selling stock	Shareholders selling stock
3. Prior funding	From established venture capital firms	Little or no funding from such sources
4. Valuation	Reasonable post offering valuation	Too high a valuation
5. Equity arrangement	Equitable for new investors	Inequitable arrangement
6. Quality of underwriter	Highly regarded underwriters	Not highly regarded

In reviewing the numerous prospectuses, we observed that it was rare to find a company that displayed *only* "turnons" or *only* "turnoffs"; rather, we found that companies generally displayed some of both. However, we also observed that those companies with several turnons tended to outperform significantly those companies with several turnoffs.

After examining over one hundred prospectuses of both "high performing" and "low performing" companies, we noted that certain factors were more important than others. Consequently, we have taken into account the *relative* importance of the different factors. For instance, two of the more important factors were: 1. having a competitive advantage; and 2. having received prior funding from established venture capital firms. Therefore these factors were given somewhat higher "weighting" than some of the other factors in our model.

PREDICTING AFTER MARKET PERFORMANCE OF IPOs

As noted earlier, the purpose of this book is to provide you with the tools or framework to better predict the long-term stock performance of emerging growth companies. Our conclusion is that a company that demonstrates predictive factors which we have labeled turnons usually becomes a long-term success. Of course, developments can occur which retard the growth or the decline of a company as well. As noted earlier, it is important to read subsequent SEC filings (i.e., the 10–Ks, 10–Qs and 8–Ks) to determine if the turnons or turnoffs are still present for a particular company.

Thus, our goal throughout this book is not to pick stocks; rather, we demonstrate how you as an investor can use our framework to: 1. better understand the factors associated with successful and unsuccessful emerging growth companies; and 2. take actions to reduce your risks and increase your returns when investing in such companies.

A LOOK AHEAD

In the next few chapters, we will provide numerous illustrations of actual companies, highlighting how the individual investor can use information available readily to predict the performance of emerging growth companies. The chapters are arranged in the same order as the Tables of Predictive Factors presented earlier in this chapter.

PART TWO

Evaluating the *Winners* and *Losers* Based on the Predictors

CHAPTER 4

Look for a Unique Product in an Attractive Market

Product/Market—
Predictors of After-market Performance:

- **Product/Market Focus**
- **Competitive Advantage**
- **Growth**
- **Operating History**
- **Linkages**

PRODUCT/MARKET: KEY INDICATORS OF SUCCESS

Does the company have a clear focus of its market and its niche within that market?

Does the company have any distinct competitive advantages, resulting from a proprietary position, market-place acceptance, lower price, or superior performance? Does the company compete on factors other than price alone?

Has the company been around for a long time with a strong track record? Has the company demonstrated a history of sustainable high growth?

Are there strong growth prospects for the industry?

Is the company now or is it likely to become a major force in its industry?

Does the company have a strong relationship with customer suppliers and regulators?

Has the company been successful in forging key alliances or joint ventures with competitors and others?

Does the company have a relatively large customer base, rather than being dependent on a few large customers?

Apple Computer was founded in the mid 1970s by wunderkinds Steven Jobs and Stephen Wozniak. By the time Apple went public in 1980, it enjoyed a tremendous competitive advantage because of its proprietary technology. Moreover, Apple had a well-defined product line, which was attractive to hobbyists, educational institutions, and scientists.

In many respects, Apple enjoyed certain *product/market advantages* over its competitors. This advantage was attractive to venture capitalists initially, who funded Apple, and later to other investors at the time of its IPO.

Our research points out the importance placed on a company's product or service and upon the target market that is sought. We have identified the following five desirable product/market factors that are predictive of a successful emerging growth venture:

PREDICTIVE FACTOR: PRODUCT/MARKET

PRODUCT/ MARKET FACTORS	TURNONS (Associated with the "winners")	TURNOFFS (Associated with the "losers")
1. Product/market focus	Clear	Disparate, unfocused
2. Competitive advantage	Distinct advantage in technology, quality, price, etc.	Little or no advantages
3. Growth	Sustainable, high growth	Low growth, unsustainable
4. Operating history	Established company with a track record	Early stage venture
5. Linkages	Linkages with established companies	No such linkages

1. *Product/Market Focus.* There is a clear focus by a company on its target market and its niche within that market. A lack of focus often results in inefficient operations and missed opportunities.

2. *Competitive Advantage.* The company has some key strategic advantage over its competitors in terms of: a. a proprietary technology; b. an acknowledged preference by customers; c. a superior product or service; and/or d. a superior mix of price and performance.

3. *Growth.* The company has demonstrated high and sustainable growth and appears likely to continue its high growth in the future.

4. *Operating History.* The company has been successful over a number of years in building a customer base and product acceptance. Since the attrition rate of small companies is high during the first two years, we look for a company to have several years of successful operations.

5. *Linkages.* One important way that small emerging companies are able to compete successfully against much larger and better capitalized companies is by forming linkages or associations with other established companies. These linkages may take the form of joint ventures, joint ownership of stock, sharing of technologies, etc.

PRODUCT/MARKET FOCUS

We use the term *product/market focus* to assess how clearly a company has defined its strategy. When we talk about strategy, our concern is, "What business is the company in?" In other words,

- What is its product or service?
- What is its industry?
- What is its target market?

These three questions define the direction, "mission," or "scope of operations" of a business.

No company—especially an early-stage or emerging company—can be all things to all people. Thus, a *clear, sharply defined product/market focus* (or strategy) is extremely important for an emerging growth venture, or for just about any company, for that matter.

NO COMPANY—ESPECIALLY AN EARLY STAGE OR EMERGING COMPANY—CAN BE ALL THINGS TO ALL PEOPLE.

Look for Companies That Have a Clearly Defined Focus ...

Over one hundred companies in the computer and office auto-mation industries have gone public in recent years. The successful ones have succeeded in defining clearly and sometimes creating a market niche for themselves. For example, Apple Computer focused on the educational market for its product initially. Kaypro and count-less others failed in this regard.

Similarly, Sun Microsystems, a leading supplier of high perfor-mance 32-bit workstations that are used primarily by engineering, scientific, and technical markets, has a clear focus or mission. More-over, despite the fact that it was one of the pioneers in the workstation industry, Sun was a fairly well-established company at the time it went public, and it had already shipped more than 12,000 work-stations and board-level central processing units to over 750 customers. In part, Sun's mission called for an "open" architecture which provided users with a greater compatibility than with many other vendors.

... But Watch Out for Ones with Too Narrow a Focus

Having a clear and specific focus is important, but as investors in toymaker Worlds of Wonder (WOW) found out, having *too* narrow a focus could be a risky strategy. WOW focused on a single product line. That product line, a teddy bear named Teddy Ruxpin, "came to life" through an electromechanical animation technology which syn-chronized eye, nose and mouth movements to a corresponding speech pattern utilizing a preprogrammed cassette tape. WOW had positioned Teddy Ruxpin with a character background and ongoing storyline, building a product line that included related characters, storybooks, cassette tapes, clothing and various accessories around the main character. According to its prospectus, WOW believed that the marketing of the related items would help extend the life cycle of the product line. Its strategy worked for awhile, but as consumer tastes changed, WOW was left with its one product and with few buyers. The company went bankrupt the year after its IPO. Thus, while WOW had a clear and direct focus, we questioned the viability of "putting all their eggs in one basket" with a single product line—especially in the faddish and trendy toy business.

A marked contrast to WOW is Microsoft. Microsoft is impressive for many reasons, including the diversity of its products in its market niche. Although Microsoft has always been focused in its strategy of providing software products for personal computers, at the time of its IPO, it had over 40 software products available, including three operating systems. Founded in 1975, Microsoft went public in March of 1986 in a $59 million offering. By that time, Microsoft was a well established $150 million software company, whose credits included: 1. development of a Basic Interpreter; 2. development of the operating system (DOS) for all IBM PCs; 3. introduction of the Microsoft mouse; and 4. development of a variety of software programs for word processing and spreadsheet analysis. It developed a variety of software (unlike Lotus, which relied on its 1–2–3 spreadsheet program, and Ashton-Tate, which relied on its DBase database program) and was a leader in innovation, as evidenced by its introduction of the mouse and Windows, a graphical interphase. Incidentally, the first draft of our manuscript for this book was written in the Windows Write word processing program, using a Microsoft mouse. Subsequent versions utilized Microsoft's newer wordprocessing program, Word for Windows, as well as its spreadsheet program, Excel. As satisfied Microsoft customers, we appreciate the tremendous competitive advantages Microsoft products provide. Of course, had we taken the money we spent on Microsoft products and invested it in more Microsoft stock at the time that the company went public, this book would have taken longer to complete, but we would have fared quite well financially at the same time.

Look for Companies That Take Advantage of Social and Demographic Trends

In many industries it is critical to forecast future social and demographic trends. One of the reasons retailer Liz Claiborne was so successful was that it "sensed" the needs of business and professional women at a time women were entering the workforce in record numbers. The company took advantage of this emerging trend and practically created an industry around it. The result for stockholders who purchased the company at its IPO in 1981 was a 34-fold increase in the value of their stock, which was 12 times the increase in the overall market during a booming bull market—over 9 years.

Similarly, LA Gear has taken advantage of the trend towards fitness, resulting in substantial long term gains for the investors in its company. Those investors were just about as successful as the investors in Liz Claiborne; their stock appreciated by 14-fold over just a four year period since it went public in July, 1986.

COMPETITIVE ADVANTAGE

Generally, high performing emerging growth ventures have some distinct advantages over competitors. Such advantages include: 1. proprietary technology; 2. a new product feature; 3. a cost or technical advantage; 4. a brand-name recognition; 5. superior quality; 6. better performance for the money (i.e. value); or 7. some other significant benefit for the user of the product or service.

Cherish a Company with a Proprietary Technology

A proprietary position, either in the form of a copyright, trademark, patent, or some other exclusive arrangement, is extremely attractive. Two classic examples are Polaroid, with its instant printing process, and Xerox, with its "xerography" photocopying process. These are two of the strongest performing IPOs of all time over the long term.

More recently, Apple Computer displayed a proprietary technology with similar advantages. Despite numerous errors in its early stages of development, Apple was able to prosper, in large part, because the market was so forgiving of a company with such a technological advantage. Apple was successful in establishing its own proprietary operating system while others who attempted this strategy failed. Over the years, especially as IBM and IBM-clone manufacturers engaged in drastic price slashing as the competition increased, Apple, with its proprietary technology, was able to maintain its high margins and higher prices. This enhanced the company's profitability considerably and resulted in dramatic profits for its investors.

Two successful computer software companies with proprietary technologies are Autodesk and Microsoft. Autodesk benefited from its proprietary software and copyrights and from its AutoCAD trademark, which had substantial brand-name recognition. In five years since going public in June, 1985, Autodesk increased in value by

1,200%. Software king Microsoft has been almost as successful. The company developed most of its software products internally using proprietary development tools and methodology. This has enabled Microsoft to successfully capture a substantial part of the software market for both IBM-compatible and Apple PCs and to bring considerable fortunes to its investors.

A company with a proprietary technology has a *monopoly* over its competition. This is especially important for high-tech companies. Genentech was able to establish such a monopoly in the biotech industry. An early indicator of this was the fact that it had filed over 200 patent applications by the time it went public in 1980. The stock market often rewards technology leaders. In this case, those investors who purchased Genentech at the time of its IPO doubled their money *in just one day*. Much more important, however, the long term investors in Genentech realized a better than 1,000% stock appreciation by 1987, before declining after the October stock market crash.

A COMPANY WITH A PROPRIETARY TECHNOLOGY HAS A MONOPOLY *OVER ITS COMPETITION.*

The Absence of Competitive Advantages Spells Disaster

Vector Graphic Inc., like Apple, was a computer manufacturer founded in the mid-1970s. But, that might be where the similarity ends. Unlike Apple, Vector had no real competitive advantages in terms of proprietary technology. Like many other competitors, Vector designed, developed, and marketed microcomputer systems with accompanying software for small businesses. Since there were few barriers to entry, there were dozens of companies just like Vector competing for that market and for the scarce profits in the newly emerging microcomputer industry. Vector, as well as its investors, turned out to be big losers in this competitive battle.

An enviable position for any company is to be a leading player in a market which is about to experience meteoric growth. McCaw Cellular Communications was a leading player in the area of cellular communications, just as cable communication was expanding rapidly.

Companies That Spot Trends Early Have a Tremendous Advantage

Oftentimes companies can grow at a phenomenal rate by sensing changing technologies and moving with the growth of that technology. During the mid 1980s, the cable industry was just taking off. Home Shopping Network (HSN), which sells consumer goods over cable channels, was able to benefit from such growth in cable subscribers. As a result, it experienced a rapid increase in sales with this growth. Of course, HSN, just like Silk Greenhouse, Vector Graphic, WOW, and others, soon found that growth of a market alone does not guarantee long-term success. Despite a significant initial appreciation in its stock price, HSN's value eventually plummetted 90%. Thus, investors, in addition to considering the growth and the competitive product/market advantages of the company, must examine its financial condition carefully, before succumbing to the lure of a "hot" company.

Proper Timing Plays an Important Role

The example of Vector Graphic demonstrates how important timing may be for the success of an early stage venture. Earlier, we suggested that overall market conditions can affect the performance of IPOs. For example, if the stock market is depressed or suffers a sudden crash, as it did in October 1987, then a potentially strong IPO may never get out of the starting blocks. Similarly, an established competitor's strategy may jeopardize the success of a newer, emerging venture. For example, Vector Graphic learned painfully about the importance of timing (and perhaps luck) when it went public in October 1981, just months before IBM introduced its first Personal Computer. Vector expressed its uncertainty about IBM's potential impact in its prospectus stating:

> It is unknown what impact, if any, IBM's announcement and product introduction will have on the Company's business.

Unfortunately for Vector Graphic and its shareholders, the impact proved to be catastrophic. Vector filed for bankruptcy a year after going public.

Look for Companies with High Quality Products

Many unsuccessful microcomputer manufacturers have tried to compete solely on the basis of price. However Compaq's strategy was to emphasize the *quality and reliability*, rather than the price, of its product. This was an important factor for several reasons. First, since most other computer companies were competing on price, this was a way of differentiating Compaq from its competitors. Second, during the 1980s "quality and reliability" became buzz words for companies, especially in the automotive and electronics industries. This was a notion enhanced by such noted authors as Tom Peters and Bob Waterman (of *In Search of Excellence* fame), and William Ouchi (who wrote *Theory Z*), who described American companies which provided quality products and service to their customers. In large part, these books galvanized our consciousness about the importance of quality and reliability during the early 1980s. So, Compaq's timing in emphasizing "quality and reliability" proved fortuitous.

Another important feature of Compaq's business strategy was that it recognized IBM as the principal manufacturer of 16-bit personal computers. Compaq decided to build computers that were compatible to IBM's, rather than build noncompatible CPM-based machines. Not surprisingly, the companies that chose the strategy of building computers with CPM-based operating systems—Osborne and Kaypro, for example—have gone out of business, while Compaq's stock has soared.

Low Tech Companies Can Have Significant Competitive Advantages

Of course, low tech companies can also gain a competitive advantage by providing value to their customers. Membership warehouse chain Costco was successful in achieving rapid inventory turnover and high sales volumes by offering a limited assortment of national brand merchandise in a wide variety of product categories at discount prices. Its competitive strategy has been to enter new markets early and to become the dominant warehouse club in those market areas by maintaining low prices, building a membership base of high volume customers, and establishing multiple locations in larger cities. Based on its success over the years, the strategy seems to have worked exceedingly well. Costco's stock nearly quadrupled in a 4-year period since going public in 1985.

GROWTH

We have found that companies which have sustained a high level of growth in revenues, profits, and market share, typically outperform low-growth companies in terms of stock price appreciation. Often, these high-growth companies will operate in high-tech/high-growth industries, such as telecommunications, microelectronics, and biotechnology. However, successful high-growth companies have also been notable in typical low-tech/low-growth industries, such as retailing, apparel, and so forth. Moreover, some of the biggest "flops" in recent years have been high-tech/high-growth businesses—for example, Columbia Data Products, Vector Graphic, and Kaypro. Thus, we must look beyond the "hot growth industries" to the specific characteristics of a particular company within an industry to determine if it is a potential star performer.

LOOK BEYOND "HOT GROWTH INDUSTRIES" TO THE PARTICULAR COMPANY WITHIN AN INDUSTRY TO DETERMINE IF IT IS A POTENTIAL STAR PERFORMER.

Look for Companies That Are Pioneers in an Industry

Sustained earnings growth is a primary determinant of increased stock price. Earnings growth *often results* from increased sales of a company. Consequently, when sales increase rapidly, the investor can often expect the stock price to do the same. However, it will be the growth in *earnings,* rather than in sales by itself, that will dictate whether the company will be a long term winner.

SUSTAINED EARNINGS GROWTH IS A PRIMARY DETERMINANT OF INCREASED STOCK PRICE.

Assuming that a company's earnings will increase with its sales, an effective strategy for investors, then, is to look for companies with significant sales growth. Clearly, such growth is most pronounced at the inception or early stages of an industry. It is particularly attractive to see companies that have grown as a result of their ability to open up industries. This was evidenced by McDonalds in fast food, Federal Express in overnight delivery, Apple Computer in personal computers, and Genentech in biotechnology.

Opening new markets often requires taking bold risks and moving into uncharted territories. A poignant illustration of this theme is recounted by Eric Sevareid in his book, *Enterprise*.[1] Sevareid tells the story about the Czechoslovakian shoe manufacturing Bata family during the 1930s. Bata grew up in Czechoslovakia where his father owned a shoe company. When his father died in 1932, the younger Bata assumed control of the company. A few years later, when it became apparent that his country would fall to Hitler, Bata fled Czechoslovakia and opened up a factory in Canada. Today, the Bata Shoe Company sells 1/4 billion pairs of shoes per year. Thomas Bata summarized his philosophy of opening up new markets with this story:

> Two shoe salesmen were sent to a poverty-stricken country. One wired back, "Returning home immediately. No one wears shoes here." The other cabled, "unlimited possibilities. Millions still without shoes."[2]

High Tech, High Growth...

There has been tremendous growth of high-tech companies in recent years. While the story of Apple Computer is not quite as dramatic as that of the Bata Shoe Co., its growth has been more remarkable. Not only was Apple experiencing phenomenal growth in revenue in the years immediately prior to its IPO—1400% growth from 1978 to 1980—but it also was profitable during each year of its operation, as indicated by the following:

---

[1] Eric Sevareid. *Enterprise*, McGraw Hill, 1983, p. 13

[2] Ibid.

| | Year ending September 30, | | |
	1978	1979	1980
Revenues	$7,883	$47,939	$117,902
Revenue Growth (%)		508%	146%
Net Income	$ 793	$5,073	$ 11,698
Net Income Growth (%)		540%	131%

As suggested earlier, the appealing feature of Apple was not just that its revenues were increasing, but that its profits were increasing at an equally attractive rate.

... But Not Always High Profit

Of course, high growth alone may not be enough to ensure long-term success. Consider computer maker Vector Graphic, which, like Apple, was growing rapidly during the early 1980s. Although Vector's sales jumped an average of 1500% from $400,000 in 1977 to $25 million in 1981, in the years just prior to its initial public offering, it could not sustain its rapid growth and eventually filed for bankruptcy in 1985.

HIGH GROWTH ALONE MAY NOT BE ENOUGH TO ENSURE LONG-TERM SUCCESS.

The stories of the successes and failures of high growth companies in the computer industry suggest that it's not enough to invest in a company solely because it is in an attractive, visible, high-growth industry. You must assess the characteristics of the particular company in a given industry. One fast-growth company can be a tremendous success, whereas another can be a dismal failure. For example, although there was a boom in the computer industry in the early 1980s, and Apple became a success story, Fortune Systems lost 90% of its value in one year's time from 1983 to 1984.

Similarly, if an investor was turned on by the high growth and the glamour and hype surrounding the biotechnology industry in the early 1980s, he or she would have found that *most* of the companies that were touted by brokers because of their "proprietary positions" or their "technological capabilities" or their "superior product potential" never lived up to their expectations. In fact, investing in biotechnology, rather than investing in *quality* biotechnology companies (such as Genentech) turned out to be a great way to lose money over the last decade.

Beware of *Hot* Stocks in *Hot* Industries

Although we feel that there are tremendous opportunities for high growth stocks in emerging industries, we are cautious of many of those so called "hot stocks." We're referring to the ones that get mounds of favorable publicity; that every investor you come across succumbs to. Certainly, their stock prices can do well in a very short time. In fact, it is likely that they'll be high fliers from the moment that they go public; often, they'll even command a premium over the *proposed* IPO price. But, as quickly as they rise, they'll be susceptible to falling. They'll probably drop in price a lot quicker than they rose.

Witness, for example, Home Shopping Network (HSN), which, in just a year and a half, went from $3 per share at its IPO, to $47, and then back to $3 (when adjusted for stock splits). The stock was actually hottest when it was at $47 and numerous investors were buying it at that price. However, the fundamentals of the stock were so weak that it was destined to fall *throughout* its meteoric rise.

That's why it's important to look beyond the company's concept, and focus on the financial statements and other aspects of the company that will be addressed in the next few chapters. There are significant risks in investing in "hot" stocks in glamorous industries. This is particularly evident in high-tech industries where competition can be intense. For instance, the moment one computer company designs a breakthrough product, a dozen other companies will soon be spending tens or hundreds of millions of dollars designing one that can outperform it. That's less likely to occur in mundane, low-tech industries. Consequently, successful companies in unglamorous industries stand a great chance of avoiding competition and in becoming star performers. For example, Safety-Kleen, which sells solvent to clean greasy machine parts, was a ten-bagger during the decade of the 1980s and Loctite, which sells adhesives, has quadrupled during that time.

Just because a company is in a low growth industry does not mean that the company itself won't grow. Marriott, for example, was growing at 20% per year while the hotel industry as a whole was growing at the rate of only 2%. Its stock price increased by 1,200% during the 1980s, before declining in 1990, as its real estate value began dropping with the weakened economy in general.

Similarly, even if an industry grows at a fast rate, not all companies in that industry will necessarily succeed. This is especially true in technology industries, due to the nature of competition. Typically, high-tech companies beget new high-tech companies, with the newer companies becoming direct competitors of their previous employers. The result is that, within months, dozens of companies can enter an industry, and despite the 40%, 50%, 60%, or higher growth in the industry, there is a 100%, 150%, or 200% increase in the number of companies entering that industry. Consequently, there is not enough profit to go around.

In such cases, the niche-oriented companies—such as Cypress Semiconductor, and LSI Logic—may do fairly well, but the ones that lack a clear niche and which compete primarily on price (and are, therefore, less differentiated) will often suffer. Consequently, when there's a shakeout in the industry, often fast growth becomes nothing more than a precursor to failure, rather than a ticket to stardom. This is precisely what happened in the personal computer industry, as evidenced by Columbia Data Products, Osborne Computer, Vector Graphic, and Kaypro.

Signs of a Successful Retailer

The 1980s proved to be the best of times for a number of small retailers. One such company was Home Shopping Network (HSN), a television retailer, which was experiencing phenomenal growth, posting a 700% increase in revenues just prior to going public. In addition, HSN generated substantial profits, with after-tax returns in excess of 10% of sales:

| | Yr ending Dec. | | 8 mos. end Aug. | 6 mos. end Feb. | |
	1983	1984	1985	1985	1986
Revenues	3,639	10,819	11,141	8,285	63,862
Revenue Growth (%)		197%	671%		
Net Income	259	359	16	125	6,839
Net Inc. Growth (%)		39%			5371%

Yet, growth alone is not enough to guarantee long term success. As we'll see in the following chapters, there were several early indicators of HSN's impending decline, which tempered our excitement over their impressive growth record.

This is not to say that HSN is a weak company today that will continue to decline in value. Conversely, since its IPO in 1986, HSN has become a much more innovative, technologically advanced, better managed business. However, our point is that there was nothing to suggest that HSN was such a "gem" when it went public to warrant a 15-fold run-up in the price of its stock over the ensuing two years.

At the time of its IPO, HSN was a *concept* company. There was a lot of hype behind it, but the fundamentals of the company were poor. Of course, investors can invest blindly in such companies as HSN, which get all the hype. Or alternatively, they can look for specific indicators of success.

We look at two important predictors of success for retailers: 1. whether the company has a formula that has been duplicated and can continue to be duplicated; and 2. whether the company has been experiencing actual growth in sales and profits.

WE LOOK AT TWO PREDICTORS OF SUCCESS FOR RETAILERS: 1. WHETHER IT HAS A FORMULA THAT CAN CONTINUE TO BE DUPLICATED; AND 2. WHETHER THE COMPANY HAS BEEN EXPERIENCING ACTUAL GROWTH IN SALES AND PROFITS.

Wal-Mart, The Limited, and The Gap all became successful in one location, then duplicated that successful formula hundreds of times, city by city. This suggested continued growth in sales and profits, as well as continued appreciation in its stock price. Over the 1980s, the stock prices of these companies moved as follows: Wal-Mart and The Limited increased by more than 50-fold and The Gap increased by 70-fold.

The second important factor is increased sales in *existing* stores, rather than the mere building of new stores. Once the expansion and building slows down we want to know that the company will still be able to generate additional sales in its existing stores. Home Depot, one of the most successful retailers of recent times, was not only increasing its revenue by building new stores but its weekly sales *per store* had increased by 124% during the two years prior to going public.

Other Companies Succeed As Retailers Grow

As retailers have prospered during the 1980s, so have their suppliers. This was especially true for specialty retailers in the athletic industry, which benefited from the trend toward fitness awareness. Athletic shoe maker Reebok was one of the beneficiaries of this trend as it grew from a $1 million company to a $66 million company from 1980 to 1984.

Sales continued at an incredible pace in the following year. For the first four months of 1985, the year which it went public, Reebok had already generated $57 million in sales:

	1980	*Year ending December 31,* 1981	1982	1983	1984
Revenues	923	1,300	3,508	12,815	66,022
Revenue Growth (%)		41%	170%	265%	415%
Net Income	-106	-91	242	667	6,145
Net Inc. Growth(%)		NM	NM	276%	921%

[Note: NM = not meaningful; i.e., when one or both numbers is negative.]

| | 4 months ending April 30, | |
	1984	1985
Revenues	$9,193	$56,640
Revenue Growth (%)		516%
Net Income	710	6,450
Net Income Growth(%)		908%

Sensing the almost insatiable consumer appetite for stylish athletic shoes, fast-growing competitor LA Gear provided a formidable challenge to Reebok. LA Gear's revenue growth was equally impressive, with sales soaring 400% in the months shortly before it went public.

| | Yr ending Nov. 30, | | | 4 mos. ending April 30, | |
	1983	1984	1985	1985	1986
Revenues	4,489	9,007	10,687	1,713	8,460
Revenue Growth (%)		101%	19%		394%
Net Income	80	-444	333	-306	603
Net Income Growth(%)		NM	NM	NM	NM

Be Cautious...If Growth Seems Unreal, It May Be!

In analyzing any company's financial statements, we use a "believability" test. If sales growth or profit margins defy believability (or they just don't make sense), then we often lose faith, not only in the financial statements, but also in the integrity of management. We question whether the revenue was really earned or if the company used creative accounting methods to inflate the revenue and to deceive the investors. Carpet cleaning company ZZZZ Best is a good illustration of a company bent on deception. According to the numbers reported in its prospectus, growth was phenomenal, with revenues increasing from $575,000 in fiscal 1984 to $5.4 million during the first *three* months of fiscal 1986. Such rapid growth for an early stage venture is not that unusual. However, ZZZZ Best already had been in existence for five years. Why did sales *suddenly* increase so rapidly during the past year? Would this growth continue or was this a "one shot deal?" Also, who ever heard of such growth for a carpet cleaning business? Of course, as we later learned, much to the chagrin of the investors of ZZZZ Best, management was crooked and the company was fabricating those numbers contained on the financial statements.

High Growth Is Sometimes an Indicator of Potential Problems

Most IPOs are companies expanding at a rapid pace. As a result of such fast growth, these companies have an insatiable appetite for cash. Sometimes a small company that grows too rapidly puts a strain on its limited resources, resulting in chronic cash shortages and related problems. This was evident in the case of toymaker Worlds of Wonder (WOW), when it attempted to introduce *six* new products at one time in the fickle toy business. At that time they had only one product and it was real "hot." They hit *one* home-run, but what were the odds of them hitting another one or two in a row?

After the IPO

It's important to monitor the progress of a company. If it went public in 1988 while its sales and earnings were growing at a better than 100% rate, what does the company look like in 1990? In 1991? In 1992? What will enable earnings to continue to grow—not necessarily at the same rate, but at a fast rate, nonetheless? So, if you already own stock, or if you're considering purchasing from a company, read the annual reports and the 10–Ks, 10–Qs and 8–Ks to see if the company is the "same" as it was when it went public.

OPERATING HISTORY

Generally, it is prudent to invest in companies with at least several years of successful operations. There are many exciting concept companies, but until they have demonstrated a history of sales and customer satisfaction, you should avoid them.

IT IS PRUDENT TO INVEST IN COMPANIES WITH AT LEAST SEVERAL YEARS OF SUCCESSFUL OPERATIONS.

Although an early stage venture may demonstrate rapid growth during its first year or two, there is no basis for determining how successful it can be in the future. After all, an important predictor of a company's future performance is its past performance over a sustained period of time.

We have found that companies that have an established track record of success (and in the case of IPOs, this may be four or five years) generally are less risky than early stage companies. Most entrepreneurs recognize that the first year or two of a business are the toughest years.

Look for an Established Track Record of Success

Federal Express was incorporated in 1971 and began offering mail services in 1972. It had seven years of operation before it went public; it certainly was not a start-up company any longer. Similarly, retailer extraordinaire Liz Claiborne was an established company at the time it went public, with a five year history of remarkable growth in sales and profits.

Occasionally, companies go public after twenty or thirty years of stable, predictable performance. Such companies tend to be low risk and can provide attractive returns for investors. One such example is Sbarro, a family run company that had been engaged in the food service and restaurant business for approximately 30 years prior to bringing its Sbarro restaurants public in 1985.

New Product Line....But Same Established Management Team

The history of LA Gear is quite interesting. Perhaps we could use the word *trilogy* to describe the three businesses that the management of LA Gear have tried over the years. Beginning in 1979, it marketed shoe skates through company-owned retail stores in the Los Angeles area. Then in March of 1983, LA Gear commenced distributing a line of moderately priced canvas shoes, leather sandals and apparel under the LA Gear trademarks through department stores and company-owned retail stores also in the Los Angeles area. However, as sales slipped considerably the company again decided to try a new approach. In October of 1984, LA Gear began devoting its efforts to the design, development and marketing of footwear and its licensing activities. This third "business" proved to be a major success. Thus, despite the product line being new, the company and its management team were established and experienced at the time of its IPO.

Be Cautious of Early Stage Ventures

It is usually quite risky to invest in a new offering which is still in the start-up phase, since such companies often lack both an established product and a loyal customer base. Occasionally, we come across an exception that excites us, based either on the past success of its founder/management or because of the strong financial support provided by venture capitalists. One such case that turned out to be extremely successful was Cray Research, founded by Seymour Cray, an engineer who had been a Senior Vice President at Control Data, and had been a leading architect of large scientific computers for over twenty years.

LINKAGES

One reason small fledgling companies have difficulty surviving is that they lack the resources to compete effectively against larger, better-capitalized companies. A successful strategy to overcome this problem would be to form linkages or alliances with larger companies, suppliers, customers, and so forth. These linkages could be made in the form of joint ventures, equity purchases, financing arrangements, and the like. By forming such linkages, the smaller company gains access to additional resources—whether this be financial, technical, or marketing.

Sharing Technologies

Forming alliances with strong established companies often gives early stage ventures both greater financial muscle and technical assistance to overcome persistent problems and challenges during the difficult early years. Genentech certainly benefited from such alliances. It entered into a number of long-term commercial arrangements with major corporations under which Genentech developed specific products. Genentech believed its long-term competition would more than likely come from these large pharmaceutical and chemical companies. Hence, it had developed a strategy of working with several of them—including Lilly and Hoffman LaRoche—on product development and commercialization.

Such alliances benefit both the emerging venture in its immediate financial needs (thereby resulting in healthier financial statements, an important consideration for investors) and the more established company, which gains a "window on technology." Sun Microsystems, for example, benefited when it entered into an agreement with Computervision Corporation, which provided for the sharing of certain technologies.

A Competitive Edge: Developing a Strong Link with Customers

Compaq believed that one of the keys to success in the personal computer industry was to develop strong relationships with retail computer dealers. Competition for dealer shelf space is intense. However, Compaq was successful in developing important business relationships so that just before it went public in November 1983, its products were carried in over 800 dealer sales locations, including those affiliated with several national and regional chains such as Businessland, Computerland, Sears and Entre Computer.

Be Cautious of Companies That are Overly Dependent Upon a Few Large Customers

While establishing close ties with customers and other companies is important, *overdependence* on one or two large customers or suppliers could make a company quite vulnerable if that relationship should end. If half a company's sales come from a single client and then the client no longer needs service, then the company would lose *half its business.*

OVERDEPENDENCE ON ONE OR TWO LARGE CUSTOMERS OR SUPPLIERS COULD MAKE A COMPANY QUITE VULNERABLE.

Doing business almost exclusively with the government has its advantages and disadvantages. The government always pays its bills, albeit very slowly. One risk in doing business with the government is that as administration priorities and programs change, so does government funding, and this may hurt a company with substantial government contracts.

Sometimes, companies can overcome such an obstacle. For example, Atlantic Research, which received 74% of its revenues from the government in 1977, would have been hurt severely if the government were to have cut back on its defense spending. Couple this with the fact that virtually all of its contracts and subcontracts with the U.S. Government were subject to *renegotiation* under the Renegotiation Act of 1951. As it turned out, Atlantic Research later became a star performer, increasing in value by 737% from 1979 through 1986. This suggests that one or two turnons or turnoffs should not be enough reason to bet on a particular company; a more thorough analysis is needed. However, the reader should recognize that there were significant risks related to Atlantic Research.

A more extreme case was carpet cleaner ZZZZ Best, which relied on a *single client* for virtually all its revenues. Specifically, it generated 86% of its revenue and 85% of its gross profit from its insurance restoration business, from Interstate Appraisal Services. To make matters worse, it was uncertain that this relationship would continue. According to ZZZZ Best's prospectus:

> The company has no written or oral agreements with Interstate with respect to future restoration work and there can be no assurance that it will continue to direct business to ZZZZ Best. Moreover, the amount of business which Interstate can direct to the Company is dependent upon the number, nature and extent of claims resulting from damage to commercial facilities insured by companies represented by Interstate, over which the company has no control.

Of course, this was just one of the many problems that led to the decline and fall of ZZZZ Best.

In contrast, retailer Home Depot, Inc., which was not dependent on any single customer or vendor, bought its merchandise from approximately 600 vendors, and no single vendor accounted for as much as 10% of the purchases. Obviously, this factor alone was not responsible for the company's more than 70-fold increase in stock price over the decade of the 1980s; however, it was significant in that it was characteristic of Home Depot's carefully laid out long term strategy.

Be Cautious of Companies with a Poor Relationship with Suppliers

In addition to being overly dependent upon suppliers or customers, it can be a problem if a company has had a poor relationship with suppliers or customers. Worlds of Wonder (WOW) learned that having a poor relationship with suppliers and licensors can be problematic. It had a stormy relationship with Alchemy, Inc., the creator of its product, The World of Teddy Ruxpin. All of WOW's animated talking toys employed a technology that was licensed from Alchemy. The prospectus for WOW noted that the relationship with Alchemy was deteriorating as a result of a number of disputes. Also, a minority shareholder of Alchemy had filed suit against Alchemy, WOW, and the CEO of WOW. If WOW lost, the lawsuit would have a material adverse impact on the company. WOW had other potential problems as a result of its relationship with outside parties. Three of the six new products WOW was planning to introduce were created by outside designers.

These were all signals that the company was in a precarious position right around the time of its IPO. Nonetheless, investors were eager to invest in this new, exciting toy company, as evidenced by its stock doubling in value within months of its IPO. After the early hype faded, however, it was obvious that *real* problems still existed for the company. Ultimately, the company filed for bankruptcy within a year after its IPO.

Riding the Growth Curve of Customers Enhances a Company's Value

Jan Bell Marketing worked to align its fortunes with the growth of its two main customers—Sam's Wholesale Warehouse (owned by Wal-Mart) and the Price Club—from whom it was generating more than half its sales. As we've just indicated, it is risky for a company to be so reliant on one or two large clients. Nonetheless, Jan Bell's business continued increasing with each new membership club developed. Thus, as Sam's Wholesale Warehouse and the Price Club continued their remarkable growth, Jan Bell continued to grow as well. As its growth continued, so did its stock price, increasing by about 700% in just three years.

Of course, should retail sales for its key customers fall off, or should the company's financial position deteriorate, we would expect that a supplier such as Jan Bell would suffer. In fact, it would be much harder hit, since Jan Bell is not nearly as strong a household name as Price Club or Wal-Mart. Such was indeed the case for Jan Bell, whose stock price declined dramatically between 1989 and 1990.

PRODUCT/MARKET: SUMMARY POINTS

Look for companies that have a clearly defined focus ...

...But watch out for ones with too narrow a focus

Look for companies that take advantage of social and demographic trends

Cherish a company with a proprietary technology

The absence of competitive advantages spells disaster

Companies that spot trends early have a tremendous competitive advantage

Proper timing plays an important role

Look for companies with high quality products

Low-tech companies can have significant competitive advantages

Look for companies that are pioneers in an industry

Beware of "hot" stocks in "hot" industries

Be cautious...if growth seems unreal, it may be!

High growth is sometimes an indicator of potential problems

Look for an established track record of success

Be cautious of early stage ventures

A competitive edge: Developing a strong link with customers

Be cautious of companies that are overly dependent upon a few large customers

Be cautious of companies with a poor relationship with suppliers

Riding the growth curve of customers enhances a company's value

CHAPTER 5

Invest in a Quality
Management Team

**Management and Organization—
Predictors of After-market Performance:**

- **Management Team**
- **(Absence of) Related Party Transactions**
- **(Absence of) Litigation**

MANAGEMENT AND ORGANIZATION:
KEY INDICATORS OF SUCCESS

Does the company have a solid management team with the necessary educational background and experience?

Does the board of directors provide additional experience and expertise?

Does the prospectus provide complete information about management and directors?

Do the top executives demonstrate a full-time commitment to the company?

Are compensation packages to management reasonable?

Has management/founders made a financial commitment to the company? Does management have a substantial amount at risk in the form of stock—as investors do?

Has the company and its executives/directors avoided questionable related-party activity; e.g. interest-free loans?

Is the company free of material litigation?

Earlier, we contrasted Genentech and Genex, two biotechnology companies that emerged in the early 1980s. In comparing these companies we noted the significant differences regarding management experience. At Genentech, CEO Bob Swanson had a background as a manager, venture capitalist and scientist. Likewise, other Genentech officers and executives had experience as scientists, attorneys, and managers. In contrast, at Genex, management and directors were *primarily scientists*, with little if any backgrounds in management. Genex CEO Leslie Glick previously assisted in the forming of another company, Associated Biomedic Systems (ABS), and later served as its president and chief executive officer. Subsequent to Glick resigning as CEO, (yet still serving as its chairman of the board), ABS experienced significant difficulties and filed for bankruptcy.

Our research suggests that there are three desirable factors related to management and organization that are predictive of a successful emerging growth venture:

**PREDICTIVE FACTOR: MANAGEMENT
AND ORGANIZATION**

MANAGEMENT AND ORGANIZATION FACTORS	TURNONS (Associated with the "winners")	TURNOFFS (Associated with the "losers")
1. Management team	Solid management team (and directors/ scientific advisors) with appropriate experience in this industry	Weak management team
2. Related transactions	Absence of questionable (e.g. related party) transactions	Existence of transactions
3. Litigation	No lawsuits against management or the company	Existence of lawsuits

1. Management Team. A solid management team, including directors, scientific advisers, and so forth with the appropriate experience in the particular industry.

2. Absence Of Related Party Transactions. No questionable, e.g., related party, transactions.

3. Absence Of Litigation. No significant lawsuits against management or the company.

MANAGEMENT TEAM

Among the most important attributes of successful emerging growth ventures is the presence of an impressive management team, with the able guidance of a strong and knowledgeable board of directors. The management team should ideally be composed of bright, capable people, with successful records of relevant experience. The executive team should be an effective mix of backgrounds and experience in the technical, financial, operations, and marketing areas. The selection of a talented board of directors should *augment* management and provide the founding entrepreneurs with leadership, experience, and guidance.

Management Is More Important Than Technology

The success stories of technology companies have often seduced investors into believing that it is *solely* technology that is responsible for a company's success. Of course, we don't want to understate the importance of having a proprietary technology in an emerging growth market. There are countless examples of companies that have had such a competitive advantage to which we have alluded in the previous chapter, including Apple, Cray Research, and Autodesk. However, we should not overlook the fact that these same companies had superior management teams.

Our high-tech friends hate when we say this, but *technology can only get a company so far*; investors who lost money on Wedtech, Psych Systems, Vector Graphic, and Columbia Data Products can attest to this. (Similarly, as we noted in the previous chapter, such companies as The Limited, Wal-Mart, The Gap, etc. brought phenomenal returns for investors, despite the fact that they could hardly be referred to as high-tech companies with significant proprietary technologies.) Over the long term, it is the quality of the management team that enables the company to use its technological capabilities to its fullest potential.

We generally feel that venture capitalists—i.e., the investors of smaller, privately held businesses—are among the most astute investors. After all, they invest in companies in their risky early years. There is an important adage in venture capital circles: It's better to invest in a first rate management team with a second rate product, than a first rate product with a second rate management team. We feel that public investors would do well by following the advice of the venture capitalists, and therefore invest in management: The key to a company's long-term success.

---

*IT'S BETTER TO INVEST IN A FIRST RATE MAN-
AGEMENT TEAM WITH A SECOND RATE PROD-
UCT, THAN A FIRST RATE PRODUCT WITH A
SECOND RATE MANAGEMENT TEAM.*

Apple Sets the Stage in the Computer Industry. Apple Computer presents an illustration of how a management team should be assembled. Its two founders, Steven Jobs and Stephen Wozniak, were college dropouts who built their first computer in Jobs' garage (which is very similar to how Hewlett-Packard got started about forty years earlier) when they were in their early twenties. Interestingly, earlier, Wozniak had tried to interest his employer (ironically, Hewlett-Packard) with the idea. After Hewlett-Packard indicated a lack of interest he decided to team up with Jobs to form a new venture. The prototype computer that Jobs and Wozniak developed was the predecessor of the Apple computer.

The demand for the original Apple computer was too great for the young entrepreneurs to handle alone so they sought the help of two experienced managers with backgrounds in marketing and manufacturing: A. C. (Mike) Markkula, formerly vice president of marketing at Intel, and Michael M. Scott, formerly head of production at National Semiconductor. Scott took a 50 percent cut in salary to join the upstart company while Markkula invested nearly $100,000 of his own money in the venture.

Apple recognized the importance of having a management team with a broad range of experience. As such, the company combined eager young entrepreneurs with experienced professional managers from such established companies as Intel, National Semiconductor, and Hewlett-Packard beautifully. The management team also had a good mix of experience in marketing, manufacturing/operations, and finance.

Armed with experienced managers, Apple was then able to raise $600,000 from such established venture capital sources as Henry Singleton (who founded Teledyne), Arthur Rock (who earlier had invested in Teledyne, Fairchild Semiconductor, and Intel), Hambrecht & Quist, and Venrock Associates. As a result of the company's early success in attracting venture capital, Apple was seen as an attractive enough investment opportunity to raise $110 million at the time of its IPO, representing the largest IPO since Comsat raised $200 million fifteen years earlier. Since that time, Apple's stock price appreciated by 5-fold.

...And Compaq Followed. Compaq Computer is an excellent example of a company that assembled an impressive group of managers, which could later attract quality directors and venture capital support. Ultimately, this formula was vital in its growth and subsequent IPO.

Compaq's management team was a group of well-educated young managers from such outstanding companies as Texas Instruments, IBM, and Bell Laboratories. Although Rod Canion, the company's CEO, often got publicity, the company was clearly a team-oriented enterprise, with defined experience in engineering, sales, marketing, production, and finance. Compaq's founding management team was strengthened significantly by its ability to attract a board of directors that included: (chairman of the board) Ben Rosen, a well-respected venture capitalist (general partner of Sevin Rosen Management Co.) and a director of Lotus Development Corporation; L. J. Sevin, of the same venture capital firm, and a founder of Mostek; and L. John Doerr, another well-respected venture capitalist who was a partner in Kleiner Perkins Caufield & Byers, and who had previously worked at Intel Corporation and Monsanto Company. Since its IPO, Compaq's stock value increased by 5-fold in just six years.

Another computer manufacturer, Tandem Computer, had an equally impressive management team. The company was founded in 1974 by Jim Treybig, along with several other experienced managers, from Hewlett-Packard primarily. The management team was so impressive that Kleiner Perkins Caufield & Byers, the Mayfield Fund, and some of the other leading venture capital firms in the country, invested in this start-up company. Over the next ten years, Tandem's stock increased in value by nearly 40-fold. Not surprisingly, since the managers at Tandem are so highly regarded, many either have been recruited by competitors or have started their own ventures (for instance Stratus Computer).

Strong Management Teams in Supercomputers and Workstations. In the supercomputer industry, Cray Research was a widely touted IPO. This was largely due to its superb management team. The company was able to attract experienced managers from Control Data, who had impressive academic credentials, such as advanced engineering degrees from MIT, Harvard, and the University of Minnesota. Within the first two years of the company's IPO, its stock price had increased by 9-fold.

In the area of computer workstations, the top management at Sun Microsystems had equally outstanding credentials as their counterparts at Compaq and Cray. Founder and CEO Scott McNealy, who previously served as director of operations at Onyx Systems, had been a manufacturer of microcomputers. His academic training included a B.A. from Harvard and an M.B.A. from Stanford. The other executives had broad training and experience from Digital Equipment, National Semiconductor, Apple Computer, Apollo Computer, and Convergent Technologies. Sun's stock had tripled within two years of its IPO.

Computer Software Stars. In the computer software industry, Microsoft's management team included entrepreneur and founder Bill Gates and seasoned professional manager Jon Shirley. While Gates and partner Paul Allen were laying the foundation at Microsoft in the mid seventies, Shirley was sharpening his skills in sales, merchandising, manufacturing and international operations at Tandy Corporation. Microsoft recruited other members of its management team from Procter & Gamble, Apple Computer, Intel and J. Walter Thompson. They had broad experience in all important phases of management, production, sales, and finance.

From each of these examples in the computer industry, we see a pattern of successful companies that have fully developed management teams with impressive academic and work credentials. Often, the founders of these newer, emerging ventures were responsible for the growth of earlier successful emerging growth ventures; in some cases, they have been repeat entrepreneurs. For example, managers from Intel were involved in the early growth of Apple, Compaq, and Microsoft; managers from National Semiconductor were involved in the early growth of Apple and Sun Microsystems; managers from Control Data Corporation were involved in the early growth of Cray Research; managers from Apple were involved in the early growth of Sun Microsystems; and so forth.

We suggest that, when reading a prospectus, the investor should carefully assess the backgrounds and experience of both the management team and directors to determine whether they have the experience, capability, and maturity to propel the growth of the company.

Watch Out for Omissions in the Prospectus

Not all early-stage companies in the computer industry are blessed with such outstanding management teams. Although Vector Graphic had a very capable outside director in Jean Deleage (a general partner in the prominent venture capital firm of Burr, Egan, Deleage & Co.), its management team could hardly be called "high powered." At our persusal, we were concerned about the lack of detail in the prospectus related to the background of management and directors. We were told that Robert Harp (chairman) was a senior staff engineer for Hughes Research Laboratories and that Barton Gordon (director) was president of another company. However, *no* background information was presented on two key executives: Lore Harp (president and CEO; she was also the wife of Robert Harp) and Carole Ely (senior vice-president).

Likewise, the prospectus of Columbia Data Products provided little information about the background and experience of its management. Should we conclude that this information was left out intentionally, and, if so, why? We feel that investors should be concerned about the omission of key information about management. It should come as no surprise that both Vector Graphic and Columbia Data Products filed for bankruptcy shortly after going public; this should reinforce our earlier conviction of the relative importance of the management team (as compared to product) in technology ventures.

Spotting Star Managers in Low-Tech Industries

With technology companies, a typical strong management team would include three or four highly educated (Harvard, Stanford, MIT, Cal Tech, Northwestern) young managers (often in their 30s and 40s) with engineering and/or sales experience who were previously in fast-track positions at such outstanding companies as IBM, Hewlett-Packard, Digital Equipment, Intel, and Advanced Micro Devices. (And, although it's not stated specifically in the prospectus, you can imagine that they're probably the clean cut all-American types who have a 3-handicap in golf, while playing only twice a year, and who run marathons in less than 3 hours, without working up a sweat.)

When it comes to typical low-tech, low-growth industries, we look for a different type of management team. One of the top performing companies over the last decade has been Liz Claiborne, a designer of women's clothing. Unlike many high-tech companies which were managed either by a group of young entrepreneurs or scientists with advanced degrees in engineering, the executives at Liz Claiborne included seasoned veterans in the retail clothing industry. In this industry, an engineering degree from Cal Tech will not substitute for 25 years experience. Management at Liz Claiborne included Elisabeth Claiborne Ortenberg, Arthur Ortenberg, Leonard Boxer, and Jerome A. Chazen, all of whom had rich and extensive experience in the apparel industry.

Two of the most successful fast-growth retailers over the past decade have made their mark in specialty retailing: Costco, a membership warehouse chain and Home Depot, a home improvement chain. Not surprisingly, the management at both companies has been strong. Like Liz Claiborne, Costco's managers had extensive experience in the retailing and apparel business. They came from such respected companies as The Price Company, Builders Emporium, and Fed-Mart Corporation. Home Depot had put together an equally impressive management team, whose executives had substantial experience in the retailing and home improvement field. As noted earlier, Home Depot was the most successful IPO—in terms of subsequent stock price appreciation—of the past decade.

Beware of Gaps in Management Teams

Not surprisingly, some of the major disappointments in retailing in recent years have occurred at companies with major question marks in management. For example, we were concerned about the background and qualifications of the officers and directors at Home Shopping Network (HSN). They included lawyers, real estate developers, investment bankers, and certified public accountants, with little or no retailing experience for running a fast-growth $100 million a year company; there was no evidence that HSN had anything to resemble a management team with a broad range of experience in operations, marketing, or finance. Although some of the officers at

HSN had backgrounds in the cable industry, the company was clearly lacking in industry-related experience. This was in clear contrast to managers at such successful companies as Costco or Home Depot. Also, we were concerned that HSN's young, 24-year old Vice-President of Operations, who was the son of the CEO, had *no prior experience* in this industry.

In much the same fashion, although Silk Greenhouse President Jere Bradwell and Executive Vice President D. Von Adkins *had* backgrounds in merchandising and retailing according to their prospectus, there was no evidence that either one had any management experience in those areas, to say nothing about them having the experience necessary to run a multimillion dollar national retailing chain. Just like the prospectus of Vector Graphic, which was curiously nondescript in providing background information, the prospectus of Silk Greenhouse had very little information to give us confidence in the management capabilities of either founder. We regard this as a red flag. It was not surprising to see that, although Silk Greenhouse was an immediate hit despite a depressed stock market at the time (Silk Greenhouse went public shortly after the stock market crash of 1987), the company's stock came crashing down, losing 90% of its value in about a year.

It should be emphasized once again that management teams do change over time. Thus, while we had concerns about the gaps in HSN's management at the time of its IPO, we are far less concerned about the potential problem today.

Be Wary of Founders Who Lack Experience and Maturity: ZZZZ Worst

Expertise in management is derived from training, years of experience, and maturity. A close look at the management of ZZZZ Best revealed that these three elements were sorely lacking. Founder Barry Minkow (who later was sent to prison), was 20 years old at the time of the initial stock offering. Although Minkow was an experienced salesperson, it would be safe to conclude that someone his age lacked the maturity and management training needed to operate as a chief executive officer.

Moreover, there was no substantive management background or experience for any top executives of the company. In describing the upper level managers working with Mr. Minkow, the prospectus of the company left the experience of the managers up to the reader's imagination, using such statements as:

> ... he was employed by various carpet cleaning establishments prior to joining the company ...;

> ... she was employed in the telemarketing departments of various carpet cleaning companies...;

> ... owned and operated his own telemarketing consulting firm ...;

> ... owned and operated ... an independent advertising firm ...;

Such nebulous statements about the key executives of a soon-to-go-public company should be viewed as a red flag. Investors that missed these ended up losing a lot of money when ZZZZ Best went bankrupt.

Look for a Full-Time Commitment in Management

An important factor in assessing management is their full-time commitment to the company. When the chief executive officer of an emerging venture fails to demonstrate a full-time commitment, then we often have concerns about the company. At Home Shopping Network, we learned from the prospectus that CEO Roy M. Speer

> had agreed to devote more than three quarters of his business time to the management of the company.

What else was he doing? According to the prospectus, he was a partner in the law firm, Speer and Olson, which also served as the company's general counsel, and was owner-operator of a sewerage treatment and disposal company. It appeared that Mr. Speer had many other things on his plate, in addition to being the CEO of a $100 million company.

Similarly, we had some questions about the management and directors of TIE/Communications. Its executive vice president was *concurrently* a member of a law firm. Also, its president had a 50% ownership in an independent telecommunications consulting firm. How much time did these two executives spend with their other businesses as compared to with TIE? Were there any conflicts? These were some of our concerns.

Both HSN and TIE turned out to be far from stellar performers. HSN, although skyrocketing initially, later lost 80% of its value within a few months. TIE appreciated 44-fold in its first five years, only to lose 82% of its value in the next three years.

We always try to gauge how deep the "commitment" is of management in both time *and* money. In addition to the importance that we place on key executives investing their time in the venture, we also look favorably upon them investing their money in the venture. Alternatively, we view it as a turnoff when we see a management team trying to raise millions of dollars from the public, who have risked little or none of their own money during the early years of the company. Cray Research is a good example of a company with full-time executives who have *invested personally* in the company. Initially, the company financed $2.5 million in equity capital by selling stock to officers, directors, and employees. This was just one of the many indicators to reinforce our confidence in Cray's management team. As it turned out, Cray's long-term stock performance was outstanding, increasing in value by nearly 50-fold over the next nine years.

Look for Modest Compensation Packages

We feel that members of the management team should think of themselves as stockholders, rather than as merely employees. Thus, their wealth should be tied to the increased value of the company's stock directly. Entrepreneurs who pay themselves excessive salaries, bonuses or take interest free loans, are often too short-term oriented. Instead, we prefer to invest in management teams who receive *modest compensation*, thereby conserving capital for the company to grow and prosper.

We have found several outstanding companies that clearly subscribe to this philosphy. At Apple Computer, a $100 million company at the time it went public, founders Jobs and Wozniak took home salaries of less than $50,000 apiece. Similarly, the executives at Cray Research were paid modestly to conserve capital for product development and other vital projects. Seymour Cray's compensation for 1975—the year prior to Cray's going public—was $40,000. Also, this same prudent philosophy was evident at Genentech, where CEO Swanson received a salary and bonus totaling $68,000.

Of course compensation by itself will not determine if a company's stock is going to rise or fall. However, appropriate compensation, like full-time commitment, are two good signals to *reinforce* our faith in the integrity of the management team and its long-range orientation.

Beware of "Fat-Cat" Managers with Huge Bonuses

Compensation of executives should in some way be associated with the size of the company and its performance. We feel that compensation was excessive for ZZZZ Best's CEO Minkow, which included $300,000 per year salary plus $20,000 *"attributable to his use of a Company-owned automobile."*

Of course, excessive compensation is just one factor out of many that can turn out to be a "red flag." There are instances when companies have performed poorly despite modest executive salaries. There are also many instances when companies have performed exceedingly well despite lucrative compensation packages to top executives. For example, Circus Circus paid its chairman $1.2 million—or 13% of the total profits of the company—in the year prior to its IPO. This hasn't hurt the company's stock performance, which increased 7-fold in a 7-year period since going public in 1982.

More extreme is the compensation package that LA Gear offered its executives. CEO Greenberg received an annual base salary of $225,000, plus an automobile, and received an annual bonus

> equal to 2 1/2% of that portion of the company's pretax net income over $2 million but less than $12 million and 5% of that portion of the company's pretax net income over $12 million.

The bonus totaled $1.5 million in the year prior to its IPO.

In terms of bonuses, LA Gear could not quite keep pace with its arch rival Reebok. Its CEO Paul Fireman earned $1.3 million in salary and bonuses in the year prior to going public. His compensation per his employment agreement was described in the company's prospectus:

> Mr. Fireman will receive a base salary of $350,000 and will be entitled to receive an annual bonus (prorated for 1985) equal to 5% of the amount by which the Company's annual pretax earnings exceeds $20 million.

This was of concern to us in that: 1. the bonus was based on *one factor, dollars* of income; and 2. it was completely *open-ended.* That could mean that even if the company's *margins* declined or if its debt rose precipitously or if its liquidity eroded (all of which could weaken the company), Fireman could still receive an attractive bonus—if aggregate sales and profits increased.

Regardless of our concerns, LA Gear and Reebok were both big winners immediately following their IPOs, suggesting that compensation alone should not be the sole basis for rating an investment. (More recently, however, both stocks realized significant declines due to disappointing earnings.)

Incidentally, in 1990 the board of directors at Reebok finally realized that their compensation plan made little sense and voted to limit Mr. Fireman's pay to not exceed $2 million—quite a change for Mr. Fireman who had been averaging $14 million during the previous five years. Of course, we question why on earth did the board fail to realize this compensation formula was outrageous *before* 1990?

Managers Should Own Stock: When They Benefit from Their Stock Rising, So Do Investors

We like to see a substantial amount of stock in the hands of management, so that their financial stakes correspond to those of new investors. Likewise, we also prefer to see that employees, in addition to top level executives, own stock. This serves to "spread the wealth around" and also increases employee morale and commitment. Genentech endorsed this approach and created a Series B Restricted Stock for attracting and rewarding employees and consultants. On the other hand, at Columbia Data Products, the CEO held 88% of the stock at the time of the IPO while the rest of management held *almost no stock,* raising concerns about their commitment. Genentech has been the leading biotechnology company over the past decade while Columbia Data Products filed for bankruptcy shortly after its IPO.

One of the more interesting employment agreements was that of King World's Vice President Stuart Hersch. In March 1984, he acquired nearly 150,000 shares of stock, representing 3.5% of the outstanding capital stock, for a penny per share. As an incentive, he agreed to pay $175,000 to the company in the event: 1. the company's gross receipts would *not* exceed $150 million during any fiscal year ending prior to September 1, 1987; 2. the fair market value of the company as of any date prior to September 1, 1987 would *not* be at least $100 million; and 3. within 90 days after August 31, 1987, certain members of the Board of Directors believed that Mr. Hersch had not rendered services to the company in a satisfactory manner. These were some lofty targets; revenue would have had to increase 5-fold and the market valuation would have had to double over the next three years. As it turned out, the company exceeded these targets and Hersch kept his money.

Be Wary of Nepotism ...

Earlier, we discussed the problems stemming from "too many Kays and not enough pros" at Kaypro. Similarly, we were uneasy about the executives at TCBY, which included CEO Frank Hickingbotham, his 25-year old son Herren and Frank's brother-in-law Walter Winters. Despite the strong post-IPO performance of TCBY until 1990, we were concerned with the overabundance of family members and the dearth of professional managers. It appeared that young Herren, with a B.A. in finance and seven months experience as a government and municipal bond trader, lacked the credentials typically found in an Executive Vice President. Likewise, brother-in-law Walter Winters was a vacuum cleaner distributor previously; he had no previous experience in franchising or in the frozen food business. It's possible that this weakness in management finally caught up with the company. Despite a 30-fold gain in its stock price over the first seven years of being a public company, TCBY has since lost more than 80% of its value.

A more extreme example of problems arising from mixing family and business was found at Vector Graphic. When entrepreneurs fail to separate their business from their personal and family life, it can often be detrimental to both business and personal relationships. The husband-wife executive team at Vector Graphic was having serious marital problems around the time of its IPO. According to the prospectus,

> the Company has been informed that an action seeking dissolution of [the] marriage [of Mr. and Mrs. Harp] has been filed. They have both indicated that regardless of their marital status, they intend to remain with the Company and have recently entered into three year employment contracts with the Company. No

assurances can be given that either [Mr. Harp or Mrs. Harp] will
remain with the Company for such three year period.

What effect would their strained personal relationship have on
the company's operations? If there was a substantial cash settlement,
would the Harps have to sell the business? Based on the information
in the prospectus, we had many troubling concerns.

Obviously, marital problems can be a touchy issue. Certainly,
some couples resolve their differences and can even work together
after a divorce. However, we have generally found that: 1. typically,
there is greater stress for a husband-wife executive team trying to run
a fast growing company than for other teams; and 2. when there are
personal problems, such as a pending divorce, it places a greater strain
on both the marriage and on the business. In any event, we would
consider the dissolution of the Harps (the two largest stockholders of
Vector Graphic and who were planning to continue to work together)
to be a serious red flag.

... Although Some Families Can Work Well Together

Certainly, there are potential problems in family-run businesses,
as was seen with Kaypro and Vector Graphic. However, there are
many notable instances of successful family-dominated businesses.
For example, fast growing pizza restaurant Sbarro included as executive committee members the three Sbarro brothers Mario, Joseph,
and Anthony, along with their mother Carmela. Similarly, King
World Productions was run by five of the late children of Mr. and Mrs.
King. Also, Liz Claiborne has done quite well despite its being run
(up until recently) by the wife/husband team of Elisabeth Claiborne
Ortenberg and Arthur Ortenberg.

The important question to ask is: Despite the family relationship
(that often affects only two executives out of the entire management
team), is the *overall* make-up of management one in which you have
confidence? In other words, does the management team have integrity and do they, as managers (regardless if they are husband and
wife, father and son, and so forth) have the capability to foster the
continued growth of the venture? If they are the *right* people for the
job, and are not there just because they're "S.O.B.s" (that stands for
"sons of bosses"), then the investor should not avoid the investment
simply because some of the managers are related. Shrewd investors

who adhered to this philosophy experienced a 20-fold increase in the value of their stock in King World Productions and a 30-fold increase in the value of their stock in Liz Claiborne.

Look for a Strong Board of Directors

Investors expect members of the board of directors to have outstanding qualifications and experience. In many cases, an experienced board will partially offset some of the "gaps" in the management team. Typically, however, the board should strengthen an *already strong* management team by providing the company with their leadership and experience.

Successful ventures generally have several qualified "outsiders" (i.e., not members of the organization—for example, experienced business executives with strong contacts) who serve on the board. A strong board could give a start-up company instant credibility which can assist in raising early rounds of financing, a key predictor of strong post IPO stock performance.

Alejandro Zaffaroni, a Ph.D. chemist and executive vice president of Syntex, decided to invest $2 million of his own money and launch his own pharmaceutical company, ALZA (which is named after him), in Palo Alto, California. Zaffaroni recruited a prominent board of directors, who were instrumental in giving the company the *credibility* to raise $50 million (in multiple rounds of financing) while its products were still under development. ALZA, now with sales of approximately $100 million, has experienced an average increase in revenues of nearly 30% per year over the last 5 years, with an average increase in EPS of nearly 70% over that time. During the 1980s, its stock price increased over 20-fold.

Baltimore-based biotechnology company Nova Pharmaceuticals had an equally impressive group of directors complementing its strong management team. They included chairman John Lloyd Huck, former president of Merck; Solomon Snyder, a neuroscientist from Johns Hopkins Medical School who was chairman of Nova's scientific advisory council; Henry Wendt, CEO of SmithKline Beckman (a company that had invested $70 million in this venture); Ralph Gomory, recently retired chief scientist of IBM; Edward Hennessy, chairman of Allied-Signal; and former president Gerald Ford. Apparently, these influential directors were instrumental in enabling Nova to secure funding. Aside from SmithKline Beckman, Nova received early stage funding from Eastman Kodak, Marion Laboratories, and Celanese. Moreover, although Nova had yet to market a product (although several of its products were in clinical or preclinical studies), it was able to go public in 1983, without even a lab. Within two years, its stock price had increased 5-fold. Nonetheless, it takes more than having a prominent board of directors to sustain stock price appreciation. Since 1986, Nova's stock has fallen in value considerably, largely as a result of its lack of earnings.

Prominent Venture Capitalists as Directors Can Strengthen the Company Significantly

In order to gain access to external funding, oftentimes successful companies will recruit venture capitalists and other investment professionals to serve as directors. Microsoft's board included David Marquardt, general partner of Technology Venture Investors (TVI) of Menlo Park, California, who was associated with a number of venture-capital-limited partnerships.

Similarly, at Compaq Computers and Genentech, outside directors, many of whom were early stage investors, played important roles. Ben Rosen served as Compaq's chairman and Tom Perkins, who was also chairman of high-flying Tandem Computer, served as chairman of Genentech. Likewise, members of the board of Sun Microsystems included: John Doerr, a partner at Kleiner Perkins Caufield & Byers, as well as a director of Compaq Computer Corporation; and David Marquardt, of TVI.

Directors Should Add Something Valuable; Otherwise, Why Have Outside Directors?

Successful companies generally devote the necessary time to recruit top quality outside directors who could help the company. On the other hand, most companies that have failed to enlist such outside support have performed poorly. Earlier, we showed how Kaypro was lacking in quality outside directors. Likewise, the board of TCBY included no outside advisors or experts, other than a law partner in TCBY's law firm. Similarly, the board of directors of ZZZZ Best seemed to offer little, if any, synergy to the management team. These outside board members included an automobile wholesaler, a stationery and gifts manufacturer, and an associate superintendent of schools. We questioned what knowledge and skills these directors offered to an already inexperienced management team.

*   *   *

Fortunately for the investor, the backgrounds—and previous and current associations—of the officers and directors are highlighted in the prospectus. Consequently, there is ample information available by which you can determine if they provide benefit to the company.

A red flag occurs when the prospectus has a group of "no-name" managers, previously employed at "no-name" companies, that had been funded previously by some "no-name" investors and that have, as directors, a group of "no-name" advisers. If you don't recognize any of the names of people or companies mentioned in the management section of the prospectus, then you should think twice about investing in the company. After all, one of the best indicators of whether or not a company will succeed is if it has succeeded in the past. Thus, managers, advisers, and the companies with whom they have been associated should have a *proven* track record.

RELATED TRANSACTIONS

When executives engage in questionable, related party transactions, which benefit themselves, family members, or friends at the expense of other shareholders, it raises concerns about management's integrity. The SEC requires that such transactions be disclosed in a separate section of the prospectus. Thus, they are easily identifiable for any investor searching for red flags.

> *WHEN EXECUTIVES ENGAGE IN QUESTIONABLE, RELATED PARTY TRANSACTIONS, IT RAISES CONCERNS ABOUT MANAGEMENT'S INTEGRITY.*

One type of related party transaction occurs when managers or directors use a company's resources for personal purposes. Some examples of related party transactions that raise questions about the integrity of management are: 1. loans to managers and other employees at below market interest rates; 2. loans to employees for nonbusiness purposes; 3. special business relationships with family members; and 4. relationships with individuals of questionable morals.

Often, companies will have several types of such related transactions. At Genex, for example, several officers and directors received interest-free loans. Also, Genex retained a marketing consulting firm whose owner was also a Chairman of Genex. While the consulting firm may have been eminently qualified for this consulting project, a related party transaction with the Chairman of the Board certainly *raised questions* about a conflict of interest.

Beware of Companies Offering Its Executives Interest-Free Loans

We feel strongly that a company should not be in the business of providing loans or other advances to employees or directors. If a company needs a loan, it should do what most people do—go to a bank. Several of the weaker performing companies that we examined failed to heed this advice. TIE/Communications, for example, made interest-free loans to its executive officers. Similarly, the two top executives of Silk Greenhouse also had taken out non-interest bearing loans from their company, totaling nearly $200,000.

Watch Out for Leases to Related Parties

TIE/Communications is a good example of a company that had a history of questionable transactions. A number of those transactions involved leases. One such lease was with Route 8 Associates, a limited partnership in which TIE was the general partner. Route 8 Associates was organized for the purpose of purchasing the land and constructing the building to house the company's headquarters and its engineering, warehouse, and manufacturing operations. At first, we questioned why a separate entity (Route 8 Associates) was even set up. We later learned that the reason was quite obvious—to have certain tax and other benefits flow to certain executives of TIE, and *not to all the stockholders.* We prefer to see companies that have the interests of all the stockholders (both the current and future ones) in mind, rather than only a few executives.

Beware of Transactions That Are Not "Silky" Smooth

We also had serious concerns regarding the related party transactions at Silk Greenhouse. For example, the company purchased $450,000 of inventory and fixed assets from a store owned by its President Jere Bradwell, and Vice President Von Adkins. This valuation was provided by its underwriter Robertson, Colman & Stephens—certainly not the most independent source for valuing a business.

In addition, Iris & Ivy, Inc., a corporation 47.5% owned by Jere Bradwell, operated a retail gift and accessory store in Tampa that had business relations with Silk Greenhouse. Iris & Ivy purchased merchandise and borrowed nearly $100,000 from Silk Greenhouse. We were uncomfortable with the related party loans by Silk Greenhouse to Ivy & Iris. Evidently, later on, Silk Greenhouse felt that it was not a good policy, as the company noted in its prospectus:

> the company does not intend to make any loans or provide assistance in the future of Iris & Ivy, Inc.

Watch Out for Any Associations with Shady Characters

How would you feel about investing in a company which had a business relationship with someone who: 1. was being sued by someone who had lent money to your company at rates exceeding the legal limit; 2. was being investigated by the FBI; and 3. had been convicted previously of selling certain counterfeit currency? You may ask, what kind of company would be involved in this sort of relationship. Well, ZZZZ Best was involved in this sort of relationship with a man that had this very shady background. This relationship only reinforced our already negative views about the integrity of management at ZZZZ Best.

Watch Out For Quality and Quantity of Related Party Transactions

The investor should be aware of the severity of any given related transaction (for example, ZZZZ Best's dealings with a convicted felon) as well as the sheer number of related transactions. Here's where quality *and* quantity count. Since such transactions are clearly laid out in a separate section of the prospectus, they are easy to find and to draw conclusions about.

When it comes to related transactions, Home Shopping Network (HSN) and its CEO, Roy Speer, deserve special mention. Here are some examples taken from the company's prospectus:

1. HSN leased equipment from Speer's family trust.

2. HSN entered into two agreements with Interphase, Inc. (a company in which Roy M. Speer was the sole shareholder), paying monthly rentals totaling $40,000 for computer and communication equipment.

3. HSN had an agreement with Pioneer Data, Inc. (whose president and sole shareholder was Roy Speer's son, Richard) that provided computer advice, software programs, and personnel in return for 1% of the company's gross profit. In addition, Pioneer agreed to lease computer equipment to HSN at a rental of nearly $13,000 per month.

4. Interphase was retained by the company to construct a television studio for nearly $100,000.

5. HSN borrowed nearly $400,000 from Interphase at 2% above prime.

6. HSN (through its predecessor) assumed the lease of Home Shopping Medical Center (whose name was subsequently changed to Western Hemisphere Sales, Inc.), which was owned by the Speer family, for use as the company's accounting and data processing center.

7. Western Hemisphere had an agreement to sell HSN's excess and unsaleable merchandise at prices designated by HSN. HSN received a commission of 15% on the sales.

Any investor noticing all these related party transactions would be concerned about the integrity of management at HSN.

LITIGATION

Potential litigation could pose a significant threat to small emerging growth companies; losing a major lawsuit could prove to be disastrous. Not only is the cash settlement important, but the company's reputation and its product could also be in jeopardy. Assessing the severity of any pending litigation is often difficult from reading a prospectus because most companies assert that the litigation "will not adversely affect" the company. In addition, there are instances where lawsuits could be part of the everyday business of a company. Thus, we are concerned when: 1. the *dollar amount* of the lawsuit and the potential financial burden on the company could be substantial; and 2. the *nature of the pending litigation* is serious.

Beware of Pending Litigation When the Dollar Amount Is Large

There were several cases pending against Columbia Data Products in which distributors are countersuing the company for amounts exceeding $25 million—a material amount for a company that was generating only $30 million in revenues. Also, litigation surrounding Worlds of Wonder was at one time of major concern. Its lawsuit sought: 1. damages of $25 million; 2. 10% of the company's common stock; and 3. dissolution of the business relation between the company and Alchemy, Inc. (the licensor of its product). In these cases, the material amounts were so large relative to the company's sales that they signaled extreme caution in our minds.

Beware of Pending Litigation of a Very Serious Nature

In addition to questions we raised earlier about Home Shopping Network, we also found that CEO Roy Speer had legal problems in Texas back in 1982. Certain Texas banks filed Chapter 7 involuntary bankruptcy proceedings against Mr. Speer, arising out of a commercial dispute involving oil rig leasing and drilling in which Mr. Speer and two other individuals were guarantors. On petition of Mr. Speer, the proceedings were converted to a Chapter 11 (reorganization bankruptcy). Nonetheless, this raised further doubts about an already questionable reputation.

We also had questions regarding TCBY, as litigation clouded its public offering in 1984. The day following its IPO, TCBY learned that it had been named as a defendant in a trademark infringement lawsuit filed the previous day. As a result of the suit, TCBY and its underwriter asked the NASDAQ (over-the-counter stock exchange) to suspend trading of its stock and TCBY decided to withdraw the offering and to cancel all previous trades.

TCBY President Hickingbotham had previous legal problems dating back to September 1983 when he was named as a defendant alleging that he made certain false representations concerning the value of the assets of his business (unrelated to the yogurt business) sold to the plaintiff. The plaintiffs sought damages of at least $100,000 and Mr. Hickingbotham agreed to indemnify TCBY for any losses or expenses resulting from the lawsuit. These circumstances provided us with greater doubts regarding the quality and integrity of management.

Readers of ZZZZ Best's prospectus were alerted to some of its legal problems which, in part, led to its demise. As stated in the prospectus for ZZZZ Best,

> On December 20, 1985, a complaint was filed against the Company and Barry J. Minkow in the Superior Court, Los Angeles ... by Jack Catain alleging actual damages aggregating over $1,350,000 and punitive damages. The suit arose in connection with an alleged agreement entered into in August 1985 between Mr. Catain and the Company, whereby Mr. Catain agreed to provide or arrange for the financing needed by ZZZZ Best for its insurance restoration work in return for a 50% interest in all profits from such business which he alleged he had a right to receive....
>
> In an effort to terminate any claims against the Company, a Settlement Agreement was executed pursuant to which Mr. Minkow and the Company agreed to pay $670,000 over one year plus interest and Mr. Catain agreed to dismiss the lawsuit, without prejudice. A subsequent addendum to the Settlement Agreement provided for additional payments aggregating $200,000. After having made payments aggregating approximately $500,000, and on the advice of counsel, the Company and Mr. Minkow ceased making any additional payments....

This certainly should have raised a red flag to anyone considering investing in ZZZZ Best.

MANAGEMENT AND ORGANIZATION: SUMMARY POINTS

- Management is more important than the technology
- Watch out for omissions in the prospectus
- Beware of gaps in management teams
- Be wary of founders who lack experience and maturity
- Look for a full-time commitment in management
- Look for modest compensation packages
- Beware of "fat-cat" managers with huge bonuses
- Managers should own stock; when they benefit from their stock rising, so do investors
- Be wary of nepotism ...
- ...Although some families can work well together
- Look for a strong board of directors
- Prominent venture capitalists as directors can strengthen the company significantly
- Directors should add something valuable; otherwise, why have outside directors?
- Beware of companies offering its executives interest-free loans
- Watch out for leases to related parties
- Beware of transactions that are not "silky" smooth
- Watch out for any associations with shady characters
- Watch out for quality and quantity of related party transactions
- Beware of pending litigation when the dollar amount is large
- Beware of pending litigation of a very serious nature

CHAPTER 6

Strong Earnings and Cash Flow Plus Low Debt Equals a Winner

**Analysis of the Financial Position—
Predictors of Performance**

- **Statement of Income**
- **Balance Sheet**
- **Statement of Cash Flows**
- **Auditor's Report**

FINANCIAL POSITION: KEY INDICATORS OF SUCCESS

Does the company have a history of strong earnings and growth in earnings?

Will growth in earnings continue?

Does the company control its costs adequately? Are cost controls in place?

Does the company use conservative accounting principles?

Are revenues and profits likely to recur year after year?

Is the company's income primarily the result of income from operations?

PREDICTIVE FACTOR: FINANCIAL POSITION

FINANCIAL POSITION FACTORS	TURNONS (Associated with the "winners")	TURNOFFS (Associated with the "losers")
1. Earnings	Strong earnings and earnings growth	Weak earnings
2. Balance sheet and cash flows	Strong balance sheet and cash flows	Weak balance sheet and cash flows
3. Auditor's report	Audited financials with an unqualified opinion	Absence of audited financials or a qualified opinion

A BRIEF OVERVIEW

A key aspect in evaluating any emerging growth company—or any other company for that matter—is analyzing its financial position. This includes an assessment of its financial statements, accompanying footnotes, management's discussion and analysis (MD&A), and the auditor's opinion. Serious investors who carefully analyze this information will notice early warning signs of potential problems lurking on the horizon. Because of the technical aspects of reading and interpreting financial statements, we have provided a special appendix to this chapter entitled "How to Read and Interpret Financial Statements."

Our appendix includes: 1. a discussion of the purpose and structure of the Statement of Income, Balance Sheet, and Statement of Cash Flow; 2. an illustration of each financial statement; and 3. a discussion of how to analyze financial statements using ratio analysis.

For those of you who have little or no background in reading and analyzing financial statements, we suggest that you read the appendix to Chapter 6 before you read this chapter. For those of you who are experienced in analyzing financial statements, the appendix can serve as a good reference section.

* * *

After having read the appendix (or based on your previous expertise), you are now ready to begin searching for the turnons and turnoffs in the audited financial statements, the footnotes, MD&A, and the auditor's letter. When examining the financials of emerging growth ventures, we are interested particularly in the key predictors of subsequent stock market performance, as reflected by their financial statements:

1. *Statement of Income.* Strong earnings and earnings growth, both in dollars and as a percentage of revenues.
2. *Balance Sheet.* Strong balance sheet, characterized by a strong liquidity position and a low level of debt.
3. *Statement of Cash Flows.* Strong inflow of cash, particularly from continuing and recurring operations.

4. *Auditor's Report.* Audited financials, with an unqualified (or "clean") opinion.

STATEMENT OF INCOME

On the Statement of Income we focus on whether the company has demonstrated growth in both revenue and earnings (using conservative accounting principles) and whether the company has been able to control its costs.

STATEMENT OF INCOME: KEY INDICATORS OF SUCCESS

Has the company generated strong earnings and earnings growth over several years?

Will growth in earnings continue?

Have the gross profit and net profit margins been improving?

Will the gross and net profit margins continue to improve?

Does the price-earnings (P–E) ratio reflect the company's future potential?

Does the company demonstrate a strong "quality of earnings?"

Search for Companies with Strong Earnings and Earnings Growth

Generally, investors will keep their eyes glued to the "bottom line" in order to assess the earnings (in terms of dollars) and the earnings growth (i.e., the percentage growth in earnings from year to year) of a company. Apple Computer, for example, looked quite attractive at the time of its IPO. Its net income had grown by 700% over the three previous years. Similarly, Home Depot not only had experienced strong growth in sales, but it also had been quite profitable. Immediately prior to its IPO, net income soared by over 450% over the same six-month period the prior year. Apple and Home Depot turned out to be sensational long-term performers, increasing in stock value several-fold since the time they went public.

Obviously, a sign of strength would be when a company generates strong growth in revenues *and* net income. If net income is flat or declining, while revenues increase, then we have some serious concern. That is what happened at TCBY. Although sales at TCBY increased 32% and franchise revenues jumped 158% from fiscal 1982 to fiscal 1983, its net income *plunged almost 50%*. This resulted from selling and general expenses growing so rapidly that they completely wiped out the gain in revenue. It would be nice to learn what TCBY was spending all that money on. Unfortunately, the prospectus was silent in that matter. An examination of TCBY suggests that investors should be concerned not solely with dollars of earnings and earnings growth, but also with *why* earnings rose or fell.

As Earnings Increase, in Most Cases So Does the Stock Price

Why is it important to examine earnings? The answer is clear when we ask the question, what makes the price of a company's stock rise over the long term? In essence, that's the same as asking what makes a company more valuable from year to year. The answer: First and foremost, earnings is the engine that drives the *long term value* of a company.

FIRST AND FOREMOST, EARNINGS IS THE ENGINE THAT DRIVES THE LONG TERM VALUE *OF A COMPANY.*

Among newer, emerging ventures, there may be no history of earnings due to high start-up costs. This is particularly true with high-tech companies. Consequently, it can take years for the stock price to reflect the "true value" of such a company; in other words, it will appear "overvalued" in relation to its earnings. However, over an *extended period of time*, value, as reflected by earnings, will emerge. Thus, in choosing growth companies for long term investment, investors must consider the *potential* for earnings and earnings growth.

Some companies go public just after posting their first quarterly profit, without a history of strong earnings. In contrast, Sun Microsystems, which had been profitable during each full year in operation, was quite attractive. After all, if it was already profitable, then it had strong potential for continued earnings and earnings growth.

Over the long term, as earnings rise, *so does the stock price.* The Limited provides a vivid example of this relationship, as shown on the graph below:

THE LIMITED
Stock Price/EPS Movement 1980-1990

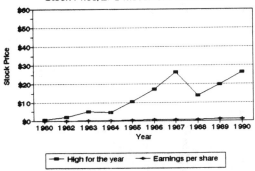

The Limited Inc.

Year	High	EPS
1980	$0.56	$0.03
1982	$2.06	$0.10
1983	$5.19	$0.20
1984	$4.69	$0.26
1985	$10.63	$0.40
1986	$17.25	$0.61
1987	$26.44	$0.63
1988	$13.94	$0.68
1989	$19.88	$0.96
* 1990	$26.56	$1.10

* (EPS includes 4th quarter estimate)

As earnings increased throughout the 1970s, so did stock price. However, when earnings fell in the late 1970s, the stock price also fell. That was followed by a few years of strong earnings—during which time the stock rose sharply—with the exceptions of 1983 and 1987, when earnings fell, and stock prices went too far ahead of earnings, eventually resulting in rapid decline of the stock.

Will the Growth in Earnings Continue?

For an emerging growth company, a central question is how can it continue to grow at a fast rate? Certainly, its growth is not likely to match its previous years' growth. However, if it does not continue to grow at a fast rate for the forseeable future, then its earnings growth is likely to slow down as well. Consequently, its value—or stock price—will be in jeopardy.

Obviously, growth can continue for a company if it has a successful product that will gain greater acceptance in the market. Consequently, the company can sell more units. Apple, Compaq, and Microsoft have proven that. Their resulting stock prices have soared as their sales and earnings have grown. Another means of growth is if a company can duplicate a successful formula in other cities. Wal-Mart, The Limited, La Quinta, and McDonald's have shown that to be true as well. As these companies have grown, their stock prices have increased by an even faster rate than the technology companies just mentioned.

The important point is that since earnings growth will generally follow from sales growth (although in the following sections we give examples of where this is *not* always the case), and since earnings usually drive up the "value" of the company—as measured by the stock price—over the long term, then sales growth is often an important predictor of long term stock performance.

Carefully Monitor the P–E Ratio

The price-earnings (P–E) ratio (or P–E multiple), which is a measure of the company's stock price relative to its earnings, is also an important determinant of its value. (We'll discuss this in greater detail in the section on "Valuation" in the next chapter.) The investor can compare the P–E ratios from company to company readily. Consequently, P–E ratios have often prompted investors to rush in to either buy or sell stocks in a given company. P–E ratios for blue chip companies have been averaging around 14 (i.e., the stock prices have been approximately 14 times the earnings of the companies) over the past few years; P–E ratios for emerging growth companies have been somewhat higher.

Price (i.e., the stock price) makes up part of the P–E ratio. The other part of the equation is reflected by earnings. As a rule of thumb, you can sometimes spot an undervalued or an overvalued stock based on its earnings growth rate as compared to its P–E ratio. If a company has a P–E ratio of 15, then you'd expect its earnings to be growing at a 15% rate; if it has a P–E of 25, then earnings should grow at a 25% rate; and so forth. Thus if the earnings growth rate is significantly greater than the P–E ratio, then the stock may be undervalued. Similarly, if the earnings growth rate is significantly less than the P–E ratio, then the stock may be overvalued. For example, Home Shopping Network (HSN) had a P–E of over 100 in 1987. Although earnings had increased dramatically from 1986 to 1987, it was unlikely that HSN could continue to grow by 100% per year for the next several years. Consequently, it should not have been surprising when its stock price came crashing down from 1987 to 1988.

IF A COMPANY HAS A P–E RATIO OF 15, THEN YOU'D EXPECT ITS EARNINGS TO BE GROWING AT A 15% RATE. IF THE EARNINGS GROWTH RATE IS SIGNIFICANTLY GREATER THAN THE P–E RATIO, THEN THE STOCK MAY BE UNDERVALUED. SIMILARLY, IF THE EARNINGS GROWTH RATE IS SIGNIFICANTLY LESS THAN THE P–E RATIO, THEN THE STOCK MAY BE OVERVALUED.

Of course, earnings may be nonexistent or exceedingly low for an emerging growth venture, due to its initial costs and lack of a customer base. Therefore, the investor should consider the likely *future* earnings, rather than merely its *current* earnings. However, the investor should also recognize that if a company has a P–E ratio of, let's say, 50 in the years prior to its IPO, then the company would have to experience an earnings growth rate of 50% for it to be fairly valued.

An important point related to P–E ratios is that the concern is not so much with current earnings, but, rather, with *future* earnings. A P–E ratio of 20 suggests that earnings will have to continue to increase by 20% to justify the premium placed on the stock price. This is especially pronounced for emerging growth companies with high—and sometimes stratospheric—P–Es. The investor should have confidence in substantial future earnings growth to justify buying stocks with high P–E ratios. For example, Microsoft's stock has been valued consistently at a P–E of over 30: yet, it has performed well enough to justify the premium that investors have had to pay to own this stock.

Look Beyond the Net Income; Beware
of Shrinking Profit Margins

When companies report their earnings for the quarter or for the year, the number that is most pronounced is the *dollars* of earnings. More important, however, are the earnings relative to sales. We are particularly concerned when the profit margins of a company—i.e., its (gross or net) profits as a percentage of sales—decline, whether for a known or unknown reason. Columbia Data Products, for example, had experienced soaring sales shortly before its IPO. However, costs had also risen rapidly and, as a result, its earnings were hurt. A sign of potential problems in controlling costs was that product costs as a percentage of sales for the period shortly before it went public jumped from 56% to 68%. Stated another way, its gross profit margins declined from 44% to 32%. Shortly after its IPO, the company went bankrupt. Contrast Columbia Data Products to Liz Claiborne, whose costs of sales as a percentage of sales *dropped* consistently each year prior to its IPO—from 73% to 63%—primarily resulting from increased purchases of imported items. Even with the meteoric rise in the stock market over the 1980s, Liz Claiborne stock actually outperformed the overall market by 1200% during that time.

Two great companies with outstanding profit margins are Microsoft and Autodesk, both high-fliers on Wall Street. The revenue growth at Microsoft had been phenomenal, climbing 44% in the year prior to its IPO and 180% over the previous two years. Yet, what made Microsoft an attractive investment opportunity was that its *net* margins were 17% of sales, or twice that of some of its leading competitors. This explains why Microsoft's total market valuation (i.e., its stock price multiplied by the number of shares outstanding, which is a fairly accurate reflection of its "true" value) is comparable to that of such megacorporations as Phillips Petroleum, Caterpillar Tractor, and ITT, even though based on revenue, Microsoft is only one-tenth to one-twentieth of their size.

Another attractive investment opportunity has been Autodesk, which was generating almost $10 million of sales around the time that it went public, but with gross profit margins at a staggering 86% and pretax profits at 29%. Couple this with the fact that Autodesk had no long-term debt and had strong cash flows from operations and you had to get excited. As it turned out, Autodesk's business continued to expand, and four short years later, its sales jumped more than 10-fold to $117 million, with gross profit margins of 90% and net profit margins of almost 28%; there are very few businesses with such margins. Not surprisingly, Autodesk's stock increased in value by nearly 12-fold in just 5 years since it went public.

Look for "Quality of Earnings"

Sophisticated analysts go beyond just reading financial statements and computing financial ratios to assess the "real" financial position and performance of a company. In so doing they:

- Evaluate the propriety of the accounting principles used
- Uncover attempts to "artificially" overstate or understate reported earnings
- Identify overstated and understated assets and liabilities
- Evaluate the degree to which earnings are backed up by cash
- Measure the degree of earnings stability
- Adjust for the effect of inflation
- Enumerate signs of future business failure
- List the financial and operating strengths of a company.

Combined, such analysis addresses, not just earnings, but the "quality of earnings" of a company. The quality of earnings encompasses more than mere understatement or overstatement of net income; it refers to such factors as stability of income statement components and maintenance of capital. For example, poor quality of earnings may be indicated when a firm has not maintained its capital properly.

It should be noted that when a company takes steps to increase its earnings artificially (in the manner we will describe in the following paragraphs), it may be reporting its earnings in accordance with the generally accepted accounting principles (GAAP). Unfortunately, GAAP provides much "flexibility" permitting companies to select their own accounting procedures. Fortunately for the investor, however, the company must report such accounting procedures and policies in the footnotes to the financial statements in its prospectus, 10Ks, annual reports, and so forth. Thus, experienced readers of financial statements recognize the valuable information gleaned from studying the accounting policy section in the footnotes. Consequently, you will be able to determine if a company is utilizing "aggressive accounting" procedures (overstating net income) and this will signal a red flag for the investor.

*   *   *

The following section points out certain cautions in reading the Statement of Income and the footnotes. One major concern in analyzing the Statement of Income relates to attempts to "overstate" or "understate" the current period's net income by shifting income or expenses from one period to the next. Among the more common examples we have found are:

- Deferring costs rather than expensing them
- Using "front end loading" of revenue
- Understating profits by "smoothing income" or taking a "big bath"
- Treating unusual nonrecurring income as ordinary income
- Using depreciation and amortization to alter profits
- Delaying or increasing operating expenses

Watch for Deferring of Costs Rather Than Expensing Them.   To prop up sagging income, some companies use a dubious technique of deferring costs (such as advertising) to create artificially high profits. This sometimes occurs in the computer and software industry, where companies can spend years developing a software program, without generating income until a product is shipped out. Sequent Computer Systems, for example, a maker of workstations, reported a 50% increase in profits for the first 9 months in 1988. The entire gain, however, was due to their decision to defer, rather than expense, $2 million of costs associated with software development.

Similarly, in fiscal 1988, LA Gear's profits jumped to $2.58 a share from 54 cents the previous year. This torrid growth continued in the first three months of fiscal 1989 as net income nearly tripled over the 1988 period from 21 cents to 62 cents. Our excitement about LA Gear's growth in profits faded quickly when we noticed that its large advertising expense was deferred and treated as an asset, rather than charged as an expense of the period. Of the total $7.2 million of advertising for the first quarter, it had deferred $3.9 million and expensed only $3.3 million. Had LA Gear expensed all the money spent on advertising (as they should have), earnings would have been about 35 cents per share, an increase of 67%; and not the reported increase of 195%. Investors who caught this aggressive accounting practice were better protected when the stock price eventually plunged. However, many investors who missed this news were hurt as the stock price declined significantly within months after the reporting of artificially inflated earnings.

Watch for Front-End Loading of Revenue. Another technique that artificially overstates profits is to record revenue before it is actually earned (known as *front-end loading*). For example, in February 1988, Jiffy Lube, the Baltimore-based franchiser of quick oil change centers, was caught *front-end loading* revenue and was ordered by the Securities and Exchange Commission (SEC) to change its accounting for franchise revenue. As a result of the change mandated, its profits declined by 75% from its reported profits. The accounting issue (which affects many franchisers) involves the problem of revenue recognition from the sale of "area development rights." These are contracts that are sold by the company granting a developer the exclusive right to open franchises in a particular territory. In return, the developer traditionally pays the company a nonrefundable fee up front. For years franchisers have been recording these up front fees as current income. But the SEC has argued that until the franchise units were open and operating, franchisers would have yet to earn the total revenue, and, thus, a portion should be deferred. Thus, this practice of front-end loading of revenues results in artificially higher reported profits than is considered appropriate.

A similar case, which first drew the attention of the SEC to this issue, involved Le Peep Restaurants' IPO filing in 1986. In its filing documents, the SEC determined that Le Peep had overstated its income from area development fees, and accordingly, the company had to revise its financial statements. As a result, the stock offering was delayed and the price was slashed by one-third.

We certainly are not asserting that it is commonplace for companies to deliberatively overstate their revenue (as Jiffy Lube and Le Peep did). However, it is common to see companies *which follow GAAP* to "front-end load" revenue. It occurs frequently with long term construction contracts when companies use the percentage-of-completion method in recognizing revenue. Under this technique, revenue is recognized, not when the money comes in or when the project is complete, but instead, in increments as the project is ongoing. This is common in high-tech companies that derive their revenue from R & D contracts (often from governmental agencies). Consider Organogenesis, a biotechnology company developing a "living skin" product for burn victims. The company was *recording* revenue of over $4 million for two long term contracts. The problem, however, was that it hadn't completed its work nor received the money. How was it able to do that? Organogenesis used the *percentage of completion method*, whereby *management* determined what percentage of the contract was completed, and recognized the revenue and expenses related to that part of the project, even if the company got no money until the work was completed. But, what happens if the company fails to complete the project, or fails to complete it within the required time or under the agreed upon conditions? That is why the percentage of completion method is considered an aggressive accounting practice that can overstate earnings.

Be Wary of Techniques for Understating Profits. Sometimes companies decide to, rather than overstate their profits, charge large expenses to the current period and to understate their profits during the current year. Don't be misled, because companies will understate their profits *if there is some benefit in the subsequent years*—like overstated profits. Two examples of the strategy of understating current profits to later benefit in the following years are: 1. smoothing of income; and 2. taking the big bath.

Smoothing Income. To cushion the blow of possible lean times in the future or to create a *smoothing* of income, some companies use an accounting technique known as a *reserve*. Reserves are created by: 1. *deliberately* charging fixed assests as repairs and maintenance; 2. *overdepreciating* fixed assets; 3. *omitting* inventory or other assets from the balance sheet; 4. *overstating* estimated or accrued liabilities or 5. *recording* fictitious liabilities on the balance sheet. Reserves also may be *unintentionally* created as follows: 1. *understatement* of inventory; 2. *overallowance* of doubtful accounts; or 3. *overdepreciation* of assets.

One classic example of the use of reserves was at Daimler-Benz, the maker of the Mercedes. When the Benz executives were questioned about the seemingly greater profits of General Motors, the

German officials replied that they used reserves as a hedge against a downturn in the auto markets. In so doing, they would have *instant* profitability to tap when the downturn occurred.

Since investors hate to see peaks and valleys in profits, companies try to accommodate by trying to smooth out these peaks and valleys. The uneven profits sometimes arise if a company introduces a new product, and, thus, sales skyrocket for one quarter. That puts pressure on the company to top that in the following year. So, many companies smooth the profits over several quarters by calling some of the windfall *special reserves*, to be used against possible future losses. (Authors and artists have this same problem; we might have one "hit" every three or four years, with the down periods being low-income years. For many years, the IRS Code recognized this factor and allowed taxpayers to use *income averaging* as a means of "smoothing" income—and tax payments—over several years.)

Taking the **Big Bath.** A second example of shifting income—or losses —from one period to another would be taking a *big bath.* A big bath refers to the practice of writing off dubious assets, when they have declined in value. Corporate management realizes that all of the costs of restructuring are grouped into one quarter, while the benefits will be realized in a later period. The reasons to take the big bath are that it enables management to cast aside old mistakes and to make themselves look good once the turnaround takes place.

A recent example of a collossal big bath took place in 1988 when AT & T decided to write off $6.6 billion of its plant assets which were becoming obsolete with the rapid change to fiber optics. As a result of the write-off, the company reported a massive loss for the year. However, it was positioning itself for "rapid profit improvement" in future periods since it had "shifted" $6 billion of expenses (what would have been depreciation on the old assets) from future periods to 1988. Removing $6 billion of expenses does wonders for your net income!

Keep Your Eye on Unusual Recurring Operating Income. Beyond keeping your eye on attempts by companies to shift income from one period to another, it's important to focus on the *usual recurring operating income* for this period. In this regard, three areas should be examined: 1. looking for unusual and nonrecurring gains or losses to adjust for them; 2. focusing on operating income (and if the company improperly classifies *nonoperating income* as part of operations, make the appropriate adjustments); and 3. being alert to gains from early extinguishment of debt.

Gains/Losses from Unusual and Nonrecurring Transactions. It is important to evaluate companies based upon their usual and recurring operations. Watch for those unusual ones, and remove them from net income in doing your analysis. Specifically, by selling an asset like real estate or a subsidiary (assuming that it has increased in value), a company will report a one-time gain, which appears on the income statement separate from operating income. Of course, that, by itself, will give the impression that the company's earnings (i.e., net income after taxes or NIAT) are substantially higher than would be the case otherwise. Consequently, the investor might fail to examine the company's operating income, which is a true measure of how the company has performed. So, the investor should exclude such one-time gains when comparing the performance of a company from one year to the next.

More extreme is the case of companies that sell such assets more regularly. Consider Prime Motor Inns, an operator of hotels and motels. The company sells property every year. It claims that such sales are a part of its normal operations, so they should not be treated as a distinct nonrecurring item. Recently, sales of property have increased (i.e., its core business), while revenues from hotel operations have been flat. The investor should recognize that Prime's method of accounting for its sales of assets is more aggressive than other companies in its industry.

Similarly, but on a much larger scale, in 1989, when RJR Nabisco suffered a 62% decrease in earnings, astute readers of the financial statements were certain not to panic, realizing that the poor showing was primarily the result of a $247 million nonrecurring charge related to its leveraged buyout. In addition, RJR Nabisco took a $55 million one-time charge as a result of writing off Premier, its unsuccessful smokeless cigarette. A similar example occurred in 1983 when Texas Instruments had a dramatic turnaround in its fortunes, posting a $6 per share loss, following a $6 gain the prior year. Again, investors may have been somewhat relieved to read that the swing was due to a one-time charge in 1983 resulting from its withdrawal from the home computer market.

Classifying Nonoperating Income as Part of Operations. In addition to being alert for nonrecurring items on the statement of income, it is important to watch for nonoperating items being comingled with operating income. Thus, when Cineplex Odeon sold off assets to fund their working capital needs and included the gain on its sale as operating income, astute readers cringed, while others were misled into thinking that the company was doing fine. While Cineplex reported pretax operating income of $44 million (which came basically from selling assets), it actually lost $14.5 million from operations.

Profits Resulting From Extinguishment of Debt. It is not uncommon to see a "gain" or "loss" related to the early extinguishment of debt, which, of course, has clearly nothing to do with usual recurring operations. One such example was when General Host reported that its pretax income from continuing operation was down 25%, but that its bottom line net income was *up 300%*. How could that happen? The answer is quite simple: The company paid off its current debt and substituted it with new debt. According to the accounting rules, when a company extinguishes its debt, any gain or loss flows into income. In this case, the swap of debt resulted in a $17 million gain, turning a poor year into a record-breaking one.

Watch for Changes in How a Company Depreciates Assets. When management falls short of its net income projections, one fairly inocuous way of "finding" additional income is to simply change an assumption related to either depreciation, warranties, bad debt write-offs, and so forth. We certainly do not suggest that a company always has a manipulative motive when it changes an assumption. However, we are saying that since the change is *unusual and nonrecurring*, you should adjust net income to evaluate a company's performance fairly as compared to other years. As an example (but on a much larger scale than our typical examples), in 1984, IBM changed from accelerated depreciation to the straight line method of depreciation for its fixed assets. This resulted in an increase in reported earnings of $375 million, merely through an accounting change, rather than through increased sales or productivity.

More recently, in a somewhat different situation, Blockbuster Entertainment, the nation's largest movie videocassette rental chain, decided to write off (i.e., depreciate) its big hits over 9 months, rather than taking the normal 2–6 years. The longer the write off period, the higher the profits. In this case, the SEC claimed that Blockbuster was too *conservative* in its accounting practice of writing off the cassettes, arguing that the 9-month write-off policy allowed the company to *understate current earnings* to the benefit of earnings in future years.

Watch for Lengthy Amortization Periods for Assets. Like depreciation, the longer a company amortizes its leasehold improvements, the higher its earnings. Cineplex Odeon, the movie theatre chain, amortized such leasehold improvements as seats, carpeting, and so forth over an average of twenty-seven years, even though it is unlikely that these assets will last that long. This is seen as an aggressive accounting practice, since it overstated Cineplex's "true" earnings. If they had amortized the leasehold improvements over a more conservative 15 years, as competitor Carmike Cinemas had done, its net income for the year 1988 would have been cut by 65% to only 54 cents per share.

Be Alert to Delays or Increases in Operating Expenses. Sometimes, sudden changes—i.e., increases or decreases—in operating expenses could signal dramatic changes in a company's financial performance. A good example is Church's Fried Chicken, a fast-food operation that had been skimping on advertising expenditures for several years. However, under new management, they decided to embark on an aggressive new marketing plan in 1984, increasing expenditures by $8.4 million over 1983. A careful perusal of the statement of income would have alerted a reader that something big was about to happen. Sure enough, the results were impressive, as earnings jumped substantially with a renewed emphasis on promotion. Shrewd investors were rewarded for their careful analysis.

BALANCE SHEET

BALANCE SHEET: KEY INDICATORS OF SUCCESS

Does the company have a strong financial condition?

Does the company have ample liquidity for normal operations?

Does the company have sufficient working capital?

Are large increases in receivables or inventory explained satisfactorily?

Does the company have a low level of debt?

Use the Balance Sheet to Predict Future Earnings

Deteriorating earnings or cash flow problems often show up on the balance sheet prior to their appearing on the statement of income. In other words, problems associated with a company's assets—for example, bloated inventories or receivables—will often result in losses in subsequent periods. This means that the balance sheet can often highlight red flags (or early warning signals) of structural problems that often lead to softening profits and a weaker subsequent performance of a stock price.

DETERIORATING EARNINGS OR CASH FLOW PROBLEMS OFTEN SHOW UP ON THE BAL-ANCE SHEET PRIOR TO THEIR APPEARING ON THE STATEMENT OF INCOME.

Many of these early warnings are especially pronounced in fast growth companies. Thus, despite the fact that fast growth companies can impress investors with their doubling, tripling, or quadrupling of sales over a short period of time, the astute investor will have the upper hand if he or she is aware of these early warning signals (which will be discussed in depth shortly) reflected on the balance sheet.

One recent example, that highlights the importance of the balance sheet as an early warning signal for weakening profits, was Digital Microwave, a manufacturer of microwave radios used in cellular and other telephone networks. In January 1990, its stock was selling for $34 a share, a 100% increase over a two-year period, reflecting substantially higher sales and profits. However, a look at the company's balance sheet revealed a far different picture. Accounts receivable had increased from 27% of sales to 45% of sales, and inventory had jumped from 45% of the cost of sales to 52% of the cost of sales over the previous year. Shortly thereafter the company's earnings came in far less than expected due to adjustments to inventory and reserves for receivables. Within months, the stock price was half of its January, 1990 value.

Look for Companies with Ample Liquidity

One sure sign of an impending financial collapse is a weakening liquidity. Liquidity is a measure of a company's ability to meet its short term obligations. A company that has barely enough current resources (assets) to cover its current obligations (liabilities) would have a problem with its liquidity. Alternatively, a company that has four times as much current assets as current liabilities (i.e., a 4:1 current ratio) likely would not have a liquidity problem, although it could be problematical in that the company may not be taking full advantage of the opportunities to invest its idle funds. However, this rarely is the case for fast growth IPOs, which tend to be cash poor.

Earlier, we compared Genentech to Genex. A further comparison can be made of their liquidity positions. Often, lack of cash, resulting from too much debt or too rapid expansion can stymie a small company's dreams of successful growth. Fortunately for Genentech and its early stockholders, the company had an ample source of cash (thanks to the early infusion of capital from the venture capitalists, the $36 million proceeds from the IPO, and the lack of any long-term debt). The company had $12 million in current assets, of which over $10 million of it was in cash and equivalents. Of its current liabilities of $3 million, only $700,000 would require any outlay of cash. In fact, the current ratio (before including the cash from the IPO) was 5.7 to 1, demonstrating an extremely liquid position for a company at this early stage of development.

In contrast, an examination of the balance sheet of Genex provided some interesting information and raised some important concerns. Specifically, its current assets, which totaled $3.9 million, included "Notes receivable—related party" of $2.6 million, but *only $92,000 in cash.* Unfortunately its current liabilities totaled about $3 million, including over $1 million on a note that was about to come due. Its current ratio of 1.5 to 1 was much more problematical than Genentech's 5.7 to 1. Ultimately, the stock performance of these two companies was just as much of a contrast as their current ratios.

Monitor Working Capital. Another measure of liquidity is working capital—the excess of current assets over current liabilities. To go along with all its other problems, ZZZZ Best had a negative working capital (its current liabilities exceeded its current assets) in the year prior to its IPO. We also had some concerns about the poor working capital position of Home Shopping Network (HSN) with current assets of $14.8 million and current liabilities of $14.2 million. In part, its liquidity weakened as a result of a dramatic increase in accounts payable (which increased from $1.7 million to $6.4 million) and in income taxes payable (which increased from $77,000 to $5.7 million). As noted, ZZZZ Best became a total flop and HSN, although rising significantly in its early years, has not been kind to investors ever since.

Although TCBY's stock performed quite well shortly after going public, we saw several problems with its financial statements that indicated a potential for major problems over the long-term. Based on the financial statements of TCBY, it is hard to imagine how any banker would lend the company money. (Perhaps that is the reason why TCBY decided to go public.) TCBY's assets totaled $1 million, yet its liabilities totaled over $3.6 million.

There were more question marks regarding TCBY's financial position. Its balance sheet showed total assets of $4.6 million, total liabilities of $4.1 million and stockholders' equity (the excess assets over liabilities) of $0.5 million. At first glance, this didn't appear to be a major problem. However, included in the total assets was the *intangible* asset goodwill totaling $1.9 million. If you removed goodwill and only considered *tangible* assets, the total assets plummeted from $4.5 million to $2.6 million and stockholders' equity disappeared, going from $0.5 million to a *negative* $1.5 million.

Watch Out for Unusual or Unexplained Increases in Accounts Receivable or Inventory

A relatively simple approach to use in assessing an impending softening in profits is to monitor the relative change in receivables and inventory in relation to the change in revenues for the same time period.

Receivables. When sales are increasing rapidly, then it is normal to see a comparable increase in accounts receivable. But what is the significance when accounts receivable are increasing at a rate two to three times greater than are sales? It suggests generally that there is a problem in collecting on the receivables, perhaps as a result of too liberal a credit policy. Also, it could indicate that customers are dissatisfied with product quality and are withholding payment until their problems are resolved. This can be an ominous sign. If the company's collections are lax, it may force the company to borrow just to meet its own liquidity needs. Inexplicably high increases in accounts receivable relative to sales could raise doubts about the quality and propriety of the reported sales. So should receivables for a particular company that are significantly greater than they are for other companies in that industry.[1] The investor should certainly monitor such developments and be cautious.

> *IF RECEIVABLES ARE INCREASING AT A FASTER RATE THAN SALES, IT CAN INDICATE THAT THERE IS A PROBLEM IN COLLECTING ON RECEIVABLES, PERHAPS AS A RESULT OF A LIBERAL CREDIT POLICY OR DISSATISFACTION WITH PRODUCT QUALITY.*

When Commodore International posted a 17% increase in sales in 1984, but receivables jumped by more than twice that amount, questions were raised about an impending cash flow crunch. Similarly, in 1988, when Cineplex Odeon's receivables jumped 262% to $152 million from $42 million the previous year, astute investors noticed a serious problem looming. Aside from the large increase, one obvious question raised was *why* a movie theater would have a large receivable. Sure enough, the increase in receivables was related to their ancillary business—"distribution sales, promotional and fee generating business." Based on its sales for the period, it was taking Cineplex *183 days* to collect on its bills, a sure sign that the company was having cash flow problems.

Inventory. If inventory rises too rapidly relative to revenues, it could indicate that the company may be getting stuck with obsolete inventory, which it will then have to sell off at a greatly reduced price. For example, at TIE/Communications for fiscal 1983, sales rose 89%

---

[1] Industry averages can be obtained from Standard & Poor's, Robert Morris Associates, etc.

but inventory jumped 157%. This trend continued the following year as sales increased 55%, while inventory spurted another 92%. With all that unsold inventory, TIE was faced with the very real probability that they would have to take substantial markdowns, unless sales grew markedly.

IF INVENTORY RISES TOO RAPIDLY RELATIVE TO REVENUES, IT COULD INDICATE THAT THE COMPANY MAY GET STUCK WITH OBSOLETE INVENTORY, WHICH IT WILL HAVE TO SELL AT A REDUCED PRICE.

We use a chart as follows to monitor these changes in receivables and inventory relative to sales:

ANALYSIS OF CHANGES IN SALES, ACCOUNTS RECEIVABLES AND INVENTORY

	Last Year	Current Year	'90–'91 % Change
Sales			
Receivables			
Inventory			

Let's consider Reebok. Although Reebok's stock did quite well initially, there were some red flags, as shown below, that could spell trouble over the years:

| | *Year ended Dec.* | | *4 mos. end April* |
	1983	*1984*	*1985*
Sales ($000)	$12,815	$66,022	$56,640
Increase in Sales (%)[2]		415%	157%
Cost of Sales ($000)	$7,288	$39,144	$33,779
Increase in Cost of Sales (%)		437%	158%
Receivables ($000)	$2,980	$15,781	$34,170
Increase in Receivables (%)		429%	550%
Inventory ($000)	$4,471	$18,358	$19,402
Increase in Inventory (%)		310%	217%
Total Current Assets ($000)	$7,520	$36,269	$55,829
Total Current Liabilities ($000)	$6,848	$31,024	$44,417
Current Ratio	1.1	1.2	1.3
Quick Ratio	0.4	0.6	0.8
Inventory/Cost of Sales	0.6	0.5	0.6

Reebok's current ratio had been slightly above 1.0 and its quick ratio had been less than 1.0. Couple this with the fact that from year end 1984 to the first four months of 1985, receivables had more than *doubled* without a corresponding increase in sales. We had some serious concerns about Reebok's liquidity.

As a general rule, we don't like to see receivables over 45 days, and certainly not over 60 days of sales (which translates into 16% of annual sales). For Reebok, receivables grew from about 20% of sales to nearly 60% of sales.

---

[2] Increases in sales, receivables, and inventory from 1984 to 1985 are annualized.

Watch for Bloated Inventories

From both a profitability and an operational standpoint, excess inventory is a problem. When a company is experiencing an unexplained increase in inventories, it can suggest that the company will be stuck with excess inventory, which eventually may have to be sold off at a significant discount. This is particularly troublesome for technology companies that face the problem of product obsolescence, whereby their inventory can virtually lose all value as new technologies develop.

Similar to receivables, it is important to monitor increases in inventories, especially in comparison to industry averages. Bloated inventories often signal that a company may have purchased too much inventory or perhaps paid too much for inventory. If the inventory is too high, it is not uncommon for future earnings to deteriorate since the company must often reduce its selling price to sell excess inventory. Analysts will compare total cost of sales to inventory and compute a *turnover ratio* which tells how frequently (how many times a year) inventory is sold. The higher the turnover the better—since no company wants to have unsold inventory in their warehouse for most of a year. For example, in 1989, Arctic Alaska Fisheries Corporation reported year end inventories equal to 19% of its cost of sales; that was double the ratio of the previous year. Stated another way, it would take the company 68 days (i.e., 19% × 360 days) to turn over its inventory. For a food processing company like Arctic Alaska Fisheries, that could "stink;" it was certainly an early warning sign of trouble.

At Reebok, we were concerned about overstocking of inventory, as evidenced by inventory growing at a faster rate than sales and cost of sales. Also, its inventory-to-cost-of-sales ratio was approximately 0.57, indicating that the company would take about 200 days to turn over its inventory. This could mean that as Reebok introduced new models, it would have to sell off its oversupply of old inventory at reduced prices, thereby resulting in reduced profits. As it turned out, this is just what took place at Reebok, which ultimately hurt its stock price.

As a general rule of thumb, we don't like to see inventories at greater than 60 days, and certainly not over 90 days of cost of sales (which translates into 25% of cost of sales). As noted, the ratio for Reebok was double that.

Watch Out for Companies That Manipulate Inventories

Companies generally report sales revenue when goods are shipped. A (very questionable) technique to prop up weak sales is to rush merchandise out of the warehouse to customers toward the end of a year (even before the sales have taken place) to record the sales revenue. A sale is recognized when an item is *shipped* to a retailer or wholesaler. Thus, some manufacturers may be tempted to just keep shipping their products during slow times, even if the retailer's shelves are overcrowded. Automobile manufacturers have been doing this for years, thereby artificially increasing their sales, while sales by the retailer may be flat.

Watch for Companies Using Aggressive Inventory Valuation

Another issue to consider when analyzing a company's quality of earnings is whether or not a conservative accounting technique is used. Normally, companies use a *last in-first out (LIFO) or a first in-first out (FIFO) valuation* to account for inventory. In most businesses, during inflationary periods (i.e., when inventory costs are rising), LIFO results in lower reported earnings for a company. (However, it results in lower taxes and higher cash flows.) FIFO, on the other hand, undervalues the rising costs of inventory and results in an artificially higher level of earnings. Thus, FIFO is considered a more "aggressive"—i.e., less desirable—inventory valuation technique. (We should point out, however, that in the case of technology companies, where component costs are often declining, LIFO is often more aggressive since it undervalues costs, thereby overstating "true" earnings.) In addition, by simply changing from LIFO to FIFO, a company can "create" instant earnings as a result of an accounting change. The difference between FIFO inventories and LIFO inventories can be substantial, as illustrated at Revere Copper and Brass. On December 31, 1980, inventories under FIFO were $90.6 million, while under LIFO they were $74.2 million, resulting in a difference of $16.4 million in profits.

While LIFO is generally thought to be more conservative than FIFO (when prices are rising), net income can still be manipulated when using LIFO, particularly in using LIFO pools. For ease in recordkeeping, similar inventory items are placed in groups (pools); each pool is treated for accounting purposes as a separate unit. The manipulation occurs when a company sets up many pools, or pools whose layers are easy to manipulate. To increase net income, older layers are eliminated, charging earlier (and lower-cost) inventory against current revenue. Thus a company has the "choice" of what layer or pool to record as the expense during a given period. This is an excellent opportunity to manipulate net income. Consider Stauffer Chemical's decision in 1982 to increase the number of its LIFO pools from 8 to 280. The action increased the company's profits by $16.5 million (or 15%). Although Stauffer justified its new method as "achieving a better matching of cost and revenue," the SEC alleged that some of the pools were *inappropriate* and that Stauffer sought *to increase* net income by using an accounting method *not in accordance with GAAP*.

Be Attentive to Insufficient Solvency

Even if a company has a product that is reasonably successful, excessive debt and insufficient solvency can be signals of a troubled company. Solvency (or leverage) is a measure of a company's ability to meet its debt obligations, including interest and principal, when due. Analysts typically compare the amount of debt (i.e., liabilities or obligations) with the amount of equity (i.e., owners' contributions). An easy way to think of debt and equity is that, *combined*, they represent the total amount the company has invested to acquire the assets (or resources) of the company. The debt represents the borrowed portion and the equity represents the portion contributed by the owners or investors. In accounting terms, the equation is:

$$\text{Assets} = \text{Liabilities} + \text{Owner's Equity}$$
$$\text{or}$$
$$\text{Total Resources} = \text{Amount Financed by Borrowing} + \text{Amount Financed by Owners}$$

Too much debt is a signal that the company may be overextended and could default—a risky situation. Consider GCA, a volatile high-tech stock that declined from $20 to $12 in late 1985 amidst a downturn in its industry. That, by itself, wasn't a problem, unless you were a shareholder who paid $20 per share. However, its Balance Sheet revealed that it had over $100 million in debt, almost all of which was bank debt, but only $3 million in cash. It also had $73 million in inventory, which put it in a precarious position should it be forced to sell off inventory that could become obsolete. As the downturn continued, GCA's stock declined further, reaching $0.10 per share before it was bought out.

TOO MUCH DEBT IS A SIGNAL THAT THE COMPANY MAY BE OVEREXTENDED AND COULD DEFAULT.

A troubling tendency for some young, high-growth companies is to finance their growth through increased borrowing. If growth moderates (as it inevitably does), will the company's cash flows be sufficient to cover the mounds of debt and interest? We had this question about Columbia Data Products. Specifically, the company had $9 million in debt coming due in 1984. Similarly, Vector Graphic, a company in the same industry, had a high level of debt, totaling 60% of its assets.

A high level of debt—or leverage—by itself, may not always indicate a problem. However, it can accentuate problems. Thus, leverage coupled with weak or uncertain cash flow can be disastrous, as was evidenced by Home Shopping Network (HSN), which had an unusually high level of debt at the time of its IPO.

Monitor the Debt/Equity Ratio

Analysts compare the debt-to-equity ratio to assess whether the company has a solvency problem. Above a certain level, the higher the proportion of debt to equity, the greater the concerns.

A typical large corporation may have a debt-to-equity ratio of approximately 1:3. That is, for every dollar of assets financed with debt, the owners have contributed three dollars. Stronger companies might have a debt to equity ratio of 1:10 or even 1:100. Weaker companies, on the other hand, might have more debt than equity; it is not uncommon to find debt to equity ratios of 4:1, 5:1, or even much higher.

Consider the Problem with Bank Debt

In evaluating a company's level of debt, you should be particularly concerned if there is a high level of bank debt. This should be quite obvious from the liabilities section of the balance sheet, as well as from the accompanying footnotes. In some regards, bank debt is the worst kind of debt for a company, since it may be *due on call*. The lender can demand money at the first sign of trouble. If a company cannot pay off a loan, then it may be forced to file for bankruptcy. This means that the creditors will have the first shot at the assets of the company, with often nothing left over for the shareholders—i.e., equity investors—who have a lower claim on the assets than the lenders.

Be Cautious of Companies That Fail to Generate Enough Cash to Fuel Their Growth

Companies with a massive amount of debt often have a difficult time generating enough cash to both service the debt and to invest in research and development and capital expenditures. For this reason, it is no surprise to find that a characteristic common to most successful emerging growth companies was low interest payments as a result of a low level of debt. For instance, Sun Microsystems had $115 million in sales, but an interest expense of only $1 million. Similarly, Liz Claiborne had solid financial statements, with strong cash flow, liquidity, and low debt. It had used its working capital to purchase property and equipment and to *reduce its debt*. In fact, Liz Claiborne's long-term debt was repaid before it went public and it had no capitalized lease obligations.

One measure of solvency is the *interest coverage ratio* of a company, which is the ratio of operating income to interest expense. In essence, it enables an investor to gauge how comfortably a company can cover its interest payments from its operating income. The higher the ratio, the less the concern about defaulting. Conversely, a low ratio suggests that a company may have trouble meeting its current obligations without further borrowings.

It's important to monitor the change in the interest coverage ratio from year to year in order to determine whether the company's debt position is becoming problematical. For example, we were concerned with Silk Greenhouse, whose sales increased 174%, but whose interest expense had increased 555%. According to its prospectus:

> during the past three fiscal years, the company had financed its growth primarily through bank borrowings.

During that period, its interest coverage ratio decreased from approximately 16 times to 6 times. This should have been a red flag to potential investors.

Assets Are One Measure of the Value of a Company

One last issue related to the Balance Sheet is the importance of assets when it comes to the valuation of a company. Assets, like earnings (but to a lesser extent than earnings), can be used as a measure of the *value* of a particular company.

ASSETS, LIKE EARNINGS, CAN BE USED AS A MEASURE OF THE VALUE OF A PARTICULAR COMPANY.

Assets are clearly stated in the balance sheet. The book value of a company (or its net worth) is the excess assets over liabilities. Thus, the accounting equation can be reformulated as follows:

Owner's Equity = Assets - Liabilities

Although the equation makes sense from an accounting perspective, it does not reflect correctly the *fair market value* or stock price of a company. One reason is as follows: The value of the liabilities is actual; you know the *actual* level of a company's debts, because the company has signed notes with its lenders. On the other hand, the assets may be *overstated* significantly: Excess obsolete inventory may be worthless; accounts receivable may have to be written off; machinery may be worth far less than its depreciated value on the balance sheet; and so forth. That could mean that the company may have to eventually write off some of these assets, resulting in lower earnings, which can later decrease stock price. As we indicated earlier, problems often appear on the balance sheet long before they appear on the earnings statement. At a worst case, in the eventual liquidation of a company, overvalued assets will result in those assets being sold off at a greatly reduced price, thereby further reducing the value—or stock price—of the company.

Alternatively, just like assets can be overstated, so can they be understated, as in the case of land, precious metals, or any other asset that may have appreciated over its original purchase price. Consequently, the company may be *undervalued* significantly, based on its balance sheet values, and it may represent a very good buying opportunity for an investor.

CASH FLOW

STATEMENT OF CASH FLOW: KEY INDICATORS OF SUCCESS

Does the company generate a strong cash inflow from operations?

Does the company have a cash management plan?

Does the company have strong cash controls?

Look for Companies with Strong Cash Flows from Operations

Cash flow—i.e., the net inflow (or outflow) of cash from operations, investments, and financing—can provide clues about a company's ability to continue operating. A healthy company typically reports net income, coupled with a strong net inflow of cash from its operations. Alternatively, a weak company often reports net losses, coupled with net outflows of cash from its operations. For a company which regularly has net outflows of cash from operations, it often must borrow, sell stock, and/or sell off assets to cover its cash shortfall. If a company exhibits a net outflow of cash from operations, especially over more than one period, this is a major concern and often a sign of deteriorating earnings and an overall weakened financial condition.

Look for Companies That Have a Cash Management Plan in Effect

Strong cash flow and careful cash management are important signals of a successful emerging growth company. Home Depot Inc. provides a good example of a company that managed its cash well. Cash flow generated from operations provided the company with a strong source of liquidity, as evidenced by the fact that 97% of total sales were for cash and a significant portion of its inventory financed under vendor credit terms.

Microsoft also had a very strong cash position. According to its prospectus:

> since its inception, the company has funded its activities almost entirely from funds generated from operations.

The financial statements of Microsoft provide a glimpse of, not only a highly profitable company (its net profit margins were an incredible 20%), but also a highly liquid company, flush with cash, with no long-term debt. Its current ratio was 3.5 to 1. Moreover, as noted on the cash flow statement, Microsoft was generating substantial excess cash from operations and it was plowing those funds back into its future growth and development.

In contrast, ZZZZ Best had generated over $5 million in revenues in the period just prior to going public, yet it had only $9,900 in cash (and no marketable securities) at the time of its offering.

Search for Companies with Strong Cost Controls in Place

We are always impressed when emerging companies, in addition to having an interesting idea or product, also concentrate on the nuances of management control and cash management. One company that impressed us in this regard was Jan Bell Marketing, a jewelry distributor, which sells its products to membership warehouse companies. Jan Bell, which has maintained a substantial inventory of gold bullion and gold products, sought to mitigate the effects of fluctuations in the price of gold by selling future gold contracts. In addition, Jan Bell maintained a proprietary computerized management information system to plan, operate, and control business activities. Jan Bell's stock increased 7-fold within four years of its going public.

Likewise, Costco, one of the leaders in the membership warehouse industry, recognized the need to control its costs. Its strategy focused on stocking large quantities of its best selling products and on maintaining tight controls over costs. Its 100,000 square foot warehouses had a standardized floor plan, designed for efficiency in both the use of its selling space and the handling of its merchandise. The warehouses carried only 3,700 stock keeping units (SKUs) compared with the 40,000 to 60,000 for full-line discount retailers. To reduce inventory handling costs, Costco had a limited selection of fast-selling brands and sizes.

Like Costco in the membership warehouse industry, Home Depot, a home repair merchandiser, implemented a system of cost control. Home Depot utilized an accounting information and control system to closely monitor customer orders, inventory levels, pricing, and so forth, with speed and accuracy. That data then became readily available for their managers' use. Home Depot's stock has been the best performing new issue of the 1980s.

FOOTNOTES, MD&A, AND AUDITOR'S LETTER

Beyond analyzing the statement of income, the balance sheet and the statement of cash flow, we have found key indicators of success and failure in the accompanying footnotes, management discussion & analysis (MD&A), and the auditor's letter.

**FOOTNOTES, MD&A, AND AUDITOR'S LETTER:
KEY INDICATORS OF SUCCESS**

Have the financial statements been audited?

Are the concerns of the auditors justifiable and troublesome?

Has the company retained the same auditor for a number of years?

Does the company use conservative accounting methods?

Has management given a candid and complete explanation in the MD&A?

SAMPLE OF AN AUDIT REPORT

To the Board of Directors and Shareholders of The Limited, Inc.:

We have audited the accompanying consolidated balance sheet of The Limited, Inc. and subsidiaries as of February 3, 1990, and the related consolidated statements of income, shareholders' equity, and cash flows for the years then ended. These financial statements are the responsibility of the Company's management. Our responsibility is to express an opinion on these financial statements based on our audit.

We conducted our audit in accordance with generally accepted auditing standards. Those standards require that we plan and perform the audit to obtain reasonable assurance about whether the financial statements are free of material misstatement. An audit includes examining, on a test basis, evidence supporting the amounts and disclosures in the financial statements. An audit also includes assessing the accounting principles used and significant estimates made by management, as well as evaluating the overall financial statement presentation. We believe that our audit provides a reasonable basis for our opinion.

In our opinion, the financial statements referred to above present fairly, in all material respects, the consolidated financial position of The Limited, Inc. and subsidiaries as of February 3, 1990 and the consolidated results of their operations and their cash flows for the fiscal year then ended in conformity with generally accepted accounting principles.

Coopers & Lybrand
Columbus, Ohio
February 19, 1990

Watch for Audit Reports with Qualified Opinions ...
Especially *Going Concern* Qualifications

An analysis of financial statements often begins by reading the report of the independent auditor. This report *generally* contains an *unqualified* opinion—the accountant's lingo for a clean bill of health. If the auditor had a strong *reservation* about the company's financial condition or of the fairness of the financial statements, he or she would generally "qualify" the report. This was the case with Cray Research. The auditors, Peat Marwick, Mitchell & Co., citing the fact that Cray was a development stage company lacking revenue, questioned the "recoverability" of its inventory which was dependent upon future events. Although that is not the ideal situation, it is not unusual for an early stage venture. The auditor's report in subsequent 10–Ks, however, gave Cray an unqualified opinion. Cray's performance has been superior since its IPO.

Look Out for the Absence of Recent Audited
Financial Statements

In some cases, a prospectus may contain recent financial statements that have been "reviewed" by their accountants, rather than "audited." A review is a far less detailed examination than an audit and the reviewed financial statements fail to give an opinion on the company's financial statements (which, of course, audited statements provide). TIE/Communications, for example, had a review for the nine-month period in 1979 shortly before going public. Similarly, ZZZZ Best included only a review report for its most recent quarterly financials before it went public. Their subsequent performance suggests that investors should have been cautious of this red flag.

Watch Out for Changes in Auditor or
Disagreements with Auditor

One early sign of trouble is when there is a change in auditors, especially resulting from a disagreement with the auditor over accounting principles. ZZZZ Best changed its auditor *twice* within a short period of time, just before it filed for bankruptcy. Investors could be alerted to any change in auditors by reading a company's 8–K which is filed at the SEC within five days after an auditor is terminated. Form 8–K outlines the reasons for the termination and describes any present disagreements over accounting principles.

Read the Footnotes: Look for Conservative Accounting Policies

As we've indicated earlier, the aggressive accounting practices mentioned above are all required to be discussed in the footnotes of the financial statements of a company. Thus, the investor will be well-advised to read the footnotes to determine how "real" the company's reported earnings are.

We not only carefully read the financial statements, but also the accompanying footnotes, searching for any signs of "creative" accounting or gimmicks, which not only lead us to question the validity of the financial statements, but also to question the *integrity of management*. A company that uses *conservative* accounting methods is one that we feel has integrity. Consider Apple Computer. In the controversial area of goodwill accounting, Apple wrote goodwill off over a 10 year period, which was far more conservative—i.e., more desirable—than the standard 40 years.

Conversely, the footnotes revealed an aggeessive—i.e., less desirable—approach to inventory valuation by Home Shopping Network (HSN). Earlier, we discussed the different inventory valuation methods. In the case of HSN, the company used the *specific identification method*, a controversial and rarely used method of accounting for inventory, which is more cumbersome and time consuming to use than either FIFO or LIFO. HSN's approach to inventory valuation is considered aggressive since it could enable management to manipulate both its inventory and its profit. In general, this method should only be used for slow moving, high cost merchandise—hardly the type of merchandise that HSN sold. Frankly, we were baffled as to why they used this method. This was just one more turnoff that we found in examining the desirability of investing in HSN.

FINANCIAL STATEMENT ANALYSIS: SUMMARY POINTS

- Search for companies with strong earnings and earnings growth
- As earnings increase, in most cases so does the stock price
- Carefully monitor the P–E ratio
- Look beyond net income; beware of shrinking profit margins
- Look for *quality of earnings*
- Be careful of companies that use aggressive accounting practices such as front-end loading or smoothing of profits
- Use the balance sheet to predict future earnings
- Look for companies with ample liquidity
- Watch for unusual or unexplained increases in accounts receivable or inventory
- Watch for companies that manipulate inventory
- Watch for companies using aggressive inventory valuation
- Watch for bloated inventories
- Be attentive to insufficient solvency
- Monitor the debt/equity ratio
- Be aware of the problem with bank debt
- Be cautious of companies that fail to generate enough cash to fuel their growth
- Look for companies with strong cash flows from operations
- Look for companies with a cash management plan in effect
- Search for companies with strong cost controls in place
- Watch for audit reports with qualified opinions ... especially *going concern* qualifications
- Look for the absence of recent audited financial statements
- Watch for changes in or disagreements with auditors
- Read the footnotes: look for conservative accounting policies

APPENDIX TO CHAPTER 6

How to Read and Interpret Financial Statements

- Purpose and Structure of Financial Statements
- Key Aspects to Understanding Financial Statements
- How We Use This Information

PURPOSE AND STRUCTURE OF FINANCIAL STATEMENTS

Statement of Income

The statement of income presents the profitability of a company for a specified period of time. A company's profit or net income is equal to its revenues and gains minus its expenses and losses. Thus, the statement of income reflects the following equation:

$$\text{Net Income} = \text{Revenues} + \text{Gains} - \text{Expenses} - \text{Losses}$$

Revenues (or sales) measure the inflows of net assets (that is, assets less liabilities) from selling goods or providing services. **Expenses** measure the outflows of net assets that are used up, or consumed, in the process of generating revenues. As a measure of operating performance, revenues reflect the services rendered by a firm and expenses indicate the efforts required or expended.

Gains and losses arise from sales of assets or settlements of liabilities that are only related peripherally to a firm's primary operating activity (i.e. sale of a building, retirement of debt, and so forth). These gains and losses arise when the amount received differs from the amount at which the asset or liability is stated in the accounting records. Thus, if you have a building that is on the books at $1 million and you sell it for $1.4 million, you would show a gain of $.4 million. If, instead, you sell it for $.8 million, you would show a loss of $.2 million.

The term **bottom line** refers to the *total dollars* of earnings (i.e. the net income after taxes—NIAT) for a company. Obviously, if a company is experiencing growth—i.e., its *dollars* of revenues are increasing—then it is common that earnings (in *dollars*) will also rise, as long as the company is efficient in its operations.

Notice, there are several important subclassifications within the statement of income, as follows:

1. *Gross profit* (or gross margin, when stated as a percentage of revenues)—excess net sales over cost of sales

2. *Operating income* (or profit from operation)—gross profit less operating expenses, such as selling, general and administrative

3. *Income from continuing operations*—net income after taxes, but before any noncontinuing transactions (such as extraordinary

gains or losses, effects of changing accounting principles and gains or losses related to discontinued operations)

4. *Net income* [NIAT] (or net margin, when stated as a percentage of revenue)—income from continuing operations plus or minus the noncontinuing transactions.

The following is an example of a statement of income:

STATEMENT OF INCOME	
Sales (or revenues)	xxxx
[Less] Cost of sales	xxxx
Gross profit	xxxx
[Less] Operating expenses	xxxx
Operating income	xxxx
[Plus] Other income	xxxx
[Less] Other expenses	xxxx
Pretax net income	xxxx
[Less] Income tax provision	xxxx
Income from continuing operations	xxxx
[Plus] Extraordinary gains	xxxx
[Less] Extraordinary losses	xxxx
NET INCOME AFTER TAXES (or NIAT)	xxxx

Balance Sheet

The balance sheet, or statement of financial position, presents a *snapshot* of a company's resources (i.e., its assets) and claims against those resources (i.e., its liabilities and owners' equity or capital) at a specific point in time. The asset portion of the balance sheet reports the effects of all of a company's past investment decisions. The liabilities and owners' equity portion reports the effects of all of the company's past financing decisions. Capital is obtained from both short and long-term creditors and from owners. Thus, the balance sheet reflects the following equation:

$$Assets = Liabilities + Owners' Equity$$

That is, a firm's assets or resources equal the claims against those assets' creditors and owners.

Uses of the Balance Sheet. The balance sheet provides information about the present resource base and the pattern of financing. It provides useful information on management's stewardship of invested capital and about the solvency and liquidity of a company. A review of the liabilities and owners' capital reveals the financial commitments of a company and the relative interests of the owners and creditors. Such information may have a bearing on a company's financial strength (ability to meet its long-term obligations) and its financial flexibility.

By examining the current assets and current liabilities, analysts can judge a company's liquidity (ability to meet its short-term obligations). Current assets minus current liabilities is called working capital. It is viewed as a measure of financial safety—a cushion against uncertain drains of financial resources in the future.

Limitations of the Balance Sheet. The balance sheet *does not* indicate the current value of a company's assets or the company itself. The individual assets do not necessarily correspond to the market value of each asset. Likewise, owners' equity (or *book value*) doesn't represent the market value, either. The book value represents the amount invested in the company, not amounts owners will get out of it.

Second, some elements of value of a business may never appear on the balance sheet because they cannot be expressed in dollars. A brand name that has attracted customer loyalty, and industry reputation for quality products, are examples of *unrecorded assets.*

A third limitation is that the balance sheet represents one moment in time. Seasonal factors and unusual circumstances must be considered. Even when comparative balance sheets for several years are presented, they fail to explain *why* changes occurred, particularly, related to operations. Accordingly, the statement of income and the statement of cash flows are essential complements to the balance sheet.

Note the following sample balance sheet:

BALANCE SHEET

ASSETS:
    CURRENT ASSETS:

Cash and equivalents	xxxx	
Accounts receivable	xxxx	
Inventory	xxxx	
		xxxx

    FIXED ASSETS:

Plant and equipment [net]	xxxx	
		xxxx

    OTHER ASSETS:

Investments	xxxx	
		xxxx

TOTAL ASSETS   xxxx

LIABILITIES AND OWNER'S EQUITY:
    CURRENT LIABILITIES:

Accounts payable	xxxx	
Short-term debt	xxxx	
		xxxx

    LONG TERM LIABILITIES:

Long-term debt	xxxx	

TOTAL LIABILITIES   xxxx
    EQUITY:

Preferred stock	xxxx	
Common stock	xxxx	
Retained earnings	xxxx	

TOTAL EQUITY   xxxx

TOTAL LIABILITIES
  AND OWNER'S EQUITY   xxxx

Statement of Cash Flows

The statement of cash flows reports the net cash (inflows minus outflows) from three of the principal business activities—operating, investing, and financing.

Rationale for the Statement of Cash Flows. In 1975, W.T. Grant filed for bankruptcy. For virtually all its prior years of operation, Grant had operated profitably. Despite generating net income each year, Grant continually found itself strapped for cash and was unable to pay suppliers, employees, and other creditors. The experience of Grant is not that unusual, particularly for emerging growth firms. Despite excellent earnings increases, a deteriorating cash position can create serious liquidity problems.

The following illustrates the statement of cash flows:

STATEMENT OF CASH FLOWS

Cash Flows From Operating:	
Net income	xxxx
Adjustments to net income	xxxx
	xxxx
Cash Used in Investing Activities:	
Purchase of equipment	xxxx
Sale of assets	xxxx
	xxxx
Cash Used in Financing Activities:	
Increase in borrowing	xxxx
Purchase of treasury stock	xxxx
Payment of dividends	xxxx
	xxxx
Net Increase (Decrease) in Cash	xxxx
[Plus] Cash at Beginning of Period	xxxx
Cash at End of Period	xxxx

As shown, there are three major sections on the statement of cash flows: 1. Cash from operations; 2. Cash used in investment activities; and 3. Cash used in financing Activities.

One key question addressed on the statement of cash flows is does the company generate enough cash from operations by itself or does it need to generate cash from investments (i.e., by selling off assets) and/or from financing (i.e., by issuing debt or equity issues) to meet its cash needs?

KEY ASPECTS TO UNDERSTANDING FINANCIAL STATEMENTS

Analysis of financial statements focuses on four main characteristics:

- Profitability
- Liquidity
- Solvency
- Activity (or Operational Efficiency)

Profitability Ratios

Profitability ratios measure the financial performance of a company over a period of time. There are a number of profitability ratios which analysts use including: 1. gross profit margin; 2. operating margin; 3. net profit margin; 4. return on assets; 5. return on equity; 6. earnings per share; and 7. price earnings ratio. These ratios are described in the following chart:

PROFITABILITY RATIOS

Gross profit margin = Gross profit / Sales

Operating margin = Operating profit / Sales

Net profit margin = NIAT / Sales

Return on assets [ROA] = NIAT / Total assets

ROE = NIAT / Total equity

EPS = NIAT / # of common shares outstanding

P–E ratio = Price per share of stock / EPS

Gross profit margin = Gross profit / Sales
(or gross margin)

(Measures the margin available to cover a company's operating expenses and yield a profit)

Operating margin = Operating profit / Sales

(Measures a company's profitablity from its main source of business)

Net profit margin = NIAT / Sales
(or net margin)

(Measures how much a company earns for each one dollar of sales. Thus, if a company had a net profit margin of 3%, it would earn three cents on every one dollar of sales.)

Return on assets [ROA] = NIAT / Total assets
(or Return on investment [ROI])

(Measures the return on investment of both the stockholders and creditors)

Return on equity [ROE] = NIAT / Total equity

(Measures the return on investment of only the stockholders)

Earnings per share [EPS] =
  NIAT / # of common shares outstanding

(Measures the profitability of the company accruing to common stockholders, on a per share basis)

Price/earnings ratio = Price per share of stock / EPS
(or P–E ratio or P–E multiple)

(Measures the stock market's current valuation of the company as related to the company's recent earnings. A low price/earnings ratio can indicate a company is conservatively valued; alternatively a high ratio can indicate a company that may be overvalued.)

Liquidity Ratios

Liquidity ratios indicate the amount of cash or short-term assets (such as receivables and inventory) available to the company. If the liquidity position gets too high, then the company is sacrificing profitability; if the liquidity position gets too low, then the company may not be able to meet its current obligations. Some key liquidity ratios are as follows:

LIQUIDITY RATIOS

Current ratio = Current assets / Current liabilities

Working capital = Current assets - Current liabilities

Quick ratio = (Current assets - Inventory) / Current liabilities

Inventory to net working capital = Inventory / (Current assets - Current liabilities)

Current ratio = Current assets / Current liabilities

(Measures the extent to which the claims of the short-term creditors are covered by the company's current or short-term assets)

Working capital = Current assets - Current liabilities

(Measures the excess of current resources over the current obligations. The greater the working capital, the greater is the cushion to meet any unforeseen cash requirements.)

Quick ratio = (Current assets - Inventory) / Current liabilities

(Measures the extent to which the claims of the short-term creditors are covered without it having to sell off inventory)

Inventory to net working capital = Inventory / (Current assets - Current liabilities)

(Measures the extent to which the company's working capital is tied up in inventory)

Solvency Ratios

Solvency (leverage) ratios that reflect a company's ability to meet its obligations indicate how the company finances its operations. If a company's leverage (debt) is too high, then it may be taking great risks; if it is too low, then it may be failing to take advantage of opportunities to use long-term debt to finance growth. Some examples of solvency ratios are listed in the following chart:

SOLVENCY RATIOS

Debt to assets = Total debt / Total assets

Debt to equity = Total debt / Total equity

Long-term debt to equity = Long-term debt / Total equity

Interest coverage ratio = Operating income / Interest expense

---

Debt to assets = Total debt / Total assets

(Measures the extent to which a company borrows money to finance its operations)

Debt to equity = Total debt / Total equity

(Measures the creditor's funds as a percentage of stockholders' funds)

Long-term debt to equity = Long-term debt / Total equity

(Measures the balance between a company's debt and its equity; a high financial leverage indicates a risk in meeting the principal and/or interest on the debt)

Interest coverage ratio = Operating income / Interest expense

(This comes from the income statement; it measures the number of times the operating income exceeds the fixed interest expense that must be paid. The greater the ratio, the less chance of defaulting on the payment.)

Activity Ratios

Activity ratios indicate the productive efficiency of the company. Generally, stronger activity ratios are associated with higher profitability (due to high productive efficiency). Some examples of activity ratios are:

ACTIVITY RATIOS

Inventory turnover = Cost of sales / Average inventory

Accounts receivable turnover= Sales / Average accounts receivable

---

Inventory turnover = Cost of sales / Average inventory

(Measures the number of times a company turns over all its inventory during a year. The higher the turnover the shorter the time a company has to sit with idle inventory.)

Accounts receivable turnover= Sales / Average accounts
   receivable

(Measures the number of times a company turns over all its receivables during a year. The higher the turnover, the quicker the customers are paying their bills.)

Using the Ratios

To be more useful, ratios of a company should be compared to its prior years' performance and to the performance of similar companies in the industry. Information about these ratios can be obtained from the following sources:

- *Almanac of Business and Industrial Financial Ratios* (Prentice Hall)
- *Annual Statement Studies* (Robert Morris Associates)
- *Dun's Review* (Dun & Bradstreet)

HOW WE USE THIS INFORMATION

The way that we use this information is that we reconstruct a simplified financial statement for a company, using the information provided in the prospectus (or 10–Ks, 10–Qs, 8–Ks and corporate annual report, and so forth), and then calculate the percentage increases in the various items over the prior year. We also calculate the key ratios pertaining to the financial statements. Here's how we set up the information for an income statement:

INCOME STATEMENT

| | *Years Ended* | | | | | *% change* |
	1987 1988 1989 1990 1991					*'90–'91*
Revenues						
Gross profit						
Operating income						
NIAT						
EPS						
KEY RATIOS:						
Gross margin (%)						
Operating margin (%)						
Net margin (%)						
ROA (%)						
ROE (%)						

Computer spreadsheets (for example, Microsoft Excel and Lotus 1–2–3) work wonders for this exercise. It's not surprising that the two leading spreadsheets were developed by companies that are on our list of winners. By creating a simple *template* that lists the income items, all the investor has to do is fill in the blanks. It then becomes quite apparent how the company has performed in recent years. If the revenues and earnings have both been increasing at comparable rates, then this will be obvious from the spreadsheet. Alternatively, if the revenues have been increasing by, let's say 100%, but the operating profits have been increasing at only 50% (this could be problematic), then this will also be obvious from the spreadsheet.

Let's take a look at an example. Apple Computer's earnings immediately prior to its IPO, as highlighted in its income statement, were as follows:

INCOME STATEMENT

	1977	Years Ended 1978	1979	1980	% change '79-'80
Revenues ($000)	774	7,856	47,867	117,902	145%
Gross profit ($000)	370	3,924	20,489	55,539	175%
Operat. income ($000)	57	1,550	10,174	29,328	190%
NIAT ($000)	42	793	5,073	11,698	134%
EPS	.01	.03	.12	.24	
KEY RATIOS:					
Gross margin (%)	48.0	49.8	42.7	47.1	
Operating margin (%)	7.3	19.7	21.2	24.9	
Net margin (%)	5.4	10.1	10.6	9.9	

Apple's growth in profitability was consistent with its growth in revenues, which is a very positive sign. Moreover, its gross margin, operating margin, and net margin remained very strong in the years immediately prior to its IPO.

Balance Sheet

Generally, small growth companies with prospects of continued growth in earnings are attractive investments. Conversely, those companies that are likely to have deteriorating earnings generally are unattractive investments. The important concern for investors is how to accurately predict whether a company will have *continued* growth in earnings. The balance sheet, which describes the assets, liablities, and equity (i.e., ownership position) of a company, provides the investor with some assistance in predicting earnings growth. A simplified version of the balance sheet is as follows:

BALANCE SHEET

	Years Ended	*% change*
	1987 1988 1989 1990 1991	*'90–'91*

Cash and Equivalents

Accounts Receivable

Inventory

Current Assets

Total Assets

Current Liabilities

Working Capital

Long-Term Debt

Total Liabilities

Stockholders' Equity

KEY RATIOS:

Current Ratio

Quick Ratio

Debt to Assets (%)

As with the income statement, computerized spreadsheets are ideal. It is especially important to monitor the growth in receivables and inventory relative to sales, as this could indicate potential problems in collections or overstocking obsolete inventory.

CHAPTER 7

Study the Terms of the Deal—Does It Seem Fair?

Financial Arrangement—
Predictors of After-Market Performance:

- **Use of Proceeds**
- **Selling Shareholders**
- **Prior Funding**
- **Valuation**
- **Equity Arrangement**
- **Quality of Underwriter**

**FINANCIAL ARRANGEMENT:
KEY INDICATORS OF SUCCESS**

Are proceeds from the stock offering targeted to fuel growth?

Are there few—if any—selling shareholders?

Has the company received early stage funding and the advice of an established venture capital firm?

Does the postoffering valuation appear fair?

Do the terms of the deal appear equitable for the new investors?

What has been the track record of the underwriter?

We have found that the financial arrangement—which involves how the company plans to use the funds and how reasonable and fair is the valuation of the company—is an important factor in predicting the long-range success of an emerging growth company. Those companies which had substantial subsequent appreciation in their stock price tended to display the following characteristics:

1. *Use of Proceeds.* The proceeds from the offering are targeted to fuel the growth of the company.
2. *Selling Shareholders.* There are few, if any, stockholders selling shares of stock at the time of the offering.
3. *Prior Funding.* The company has received prior funding from established venture capital firms.
4. *Valuation.* The postoffering valuation is reasonably priced.
5. *Equity Arrangement.* There is an equitable arrangement for the new public investors in the company.
6. *Quality of Underwriter.* The company is being taken public by a highly regarded underwriter with a proven track record.

PREDICTIVE FACTOR: FINANCIAL ARRANGEMENT		
FINANCIAL ARRANGEMENT FACTORS	TURNONS (Associated with the "winners")	TURNOFFS (Associated with the "losers")
1. Use of proceeds	Targeted to fuel growth	To repay debt; for general use
2. Selling shareholders	Few shareholders selling stock	Shareholders selling stock
3. Prior funding	From established venture capital firms	Little or no funding from such sources
4. Valuation	Reasonable postoffering valuation	Too high a valuation
5. Equity arrangement	Equitable for new investors	Inequitable arrangement
6. Quality of underwriter	Highly regarded underwriters	Not highly regarded

USE OF PROCEEDS

Search for Companies That Use the Proceeds from an Offering to Foster Future Growth

Since the SEC requires that companies include a separate section in their prospectus entitled *Use of Proceeds* to explain how the proceeds from an offering are intended to be spent, an investor has this information readily available. An investor should ask: Why is the company going public? It usually is highly desirable if the funds are targeted to fuel growth. On the other hand, it is less desirable when the proceeds of an offering are targeted: 1. to pay off debt; 2. to enable the top managers to "cash out" with a hefty profit; or 3. for some nebulous reason such as "general corporate purposes." However, the use of proceeds is only *one* factor used to evaluate a company. For example, Apple Computer, Compaq, and Federal Express each used a portion of the proceeds from their offerings to pay off debt. Clearly, their stock prices have performed quite well, despite that.

Nonetheless, we have found that when the proceeds from the offering are targeted primarily to fund the company's growth, that company tends to perform well. Such investments as plant expansion, research and development, and marketing offer the company what it needs most at a critical juncture—a large infusion of capital. The proceeds from Genentech's IPO, for example, were to be used for capital expenditures and to increase working capital for product research, development, and clinical programs. King World Productions planned to use the proceeds from its offering to acquire distribution rights to additional feature films and television properties, to expand into related activities in the entertainment industry and to develop products for merchandising. Similarly, Autodesk, Inc., a leading supplier of computer-aided design (CAD) software, raised over $15 million in its initial public offering, largely to expand its sales and marketing operations. In each of these cases, the companies had a *specific* purpose in mind for the funds, with the basic objective to expand operations. This looks very attractive to an investor interested in long-term growth and profitability.

WHEN THE PROCEEDS FROM THE OFFERING ARE TARGETED TO FUND THE COMPANY'S GROWTH, THAT COMPANY TENDS TO PERFORM WELL.

Be Cautious When Funding Is Targeted for Working Capital

Generally, it is less desirable, although often necessary, for companies to use the proceeds from an offering entirely for working capital purposes. This would include financing receivables, purchasing inventory, and providing additional cash for day-to-day operations. Home Shopping Network (HSN), for instance, planned to use the proceeds from the offering for acquisition of inventory, financing of receivables, expansion of a computer system, preopening expenses, and debt repayment.

We're somewhat less concerned when high-tech companies use the proceeds for working capital to support their fast growth. Microsoft, for example, planned to use the proceeds from its offering for working capital and other purposes. Similarly, Sun Microsystems used the $45 million from the initial public offering, primarily for financing receivables and inventory. This is quite common for technology companies which need to expand their inventory levels and extend credit to customers in order to meet a backlog of orders and to generate additional orders. It is important, however, to monitor changes in receivables and inventory relative to sales carefully (see section on unexplained increases in accounts receivable or inventory in the previous chapter).

Beware of Companies That Use Funding to Repay Debt...

We are often concerned when a company uses proceeds *solely* to pay off debt. In effect, the company transfers the financial risk from itself and the current shareholders to the new investors. Moreover, as noted in the section on leverage in the previous chapter, a more desirable situation would be to invest in companies that *already* (i.e., prior to an IPO, for example) have a low level of debt.

TIE/Communications, for example, planned to use its proceeds almost exclusively to pay off short-term indebtedness of nearly $2 million. Almost none of the proceeds would be used for expansion. Also, the proceeds from Silk Greenhouse's IPO were to be used largely to repay bank borrowings. Similarly, Worlds of Wonder planned to use the proceeds from its offering for repayment of subordinated debt and other short-term debt.

An even more extreme case is ZZZZ Best, which planned to use the proceeds as an alternative to debt. According to its prospectus,

> due to a number of factors the company has been unable, on its own, to obtain financing from traditional lending sources.

You don't have to read between the lines to conclude that the reason ZZZZ Best was going public was that *no one else would lend the company money.* Does this sound like the kind of company in which you would want to invest?

... But, in Some Cases, Using the Proceeds to Reduce Debt is Desirable

One specialized situation involving IPOs in which it may be desirable to use the proceeds to pay off debt is in the case of leveraged buyouts (LBOs). Such a company which had previously taken on a substantial amount of debt to go private, may be compelled to go public to help pay off some of that debt. This may be a better use of the funds (especially if it is a large, slow-growth company) than to target it for future growth. An example of such a company was Geneva Steel, an IPO which initially was rejected by the market. In fact, the market was concerned because the company planned to use the proceeds for capital improvements, rather than to pay their substantial debt. Eventually, after modifying the terms of the deal, Geneva finally did go public in a much smaller offering.

SELLING SHAREHOLDERS

Insider Buying, Insider Selling

For large companies, we often hear of "insider selling" or "insider buying," which refers to officers and/or directors selling or buying shares of stock in their company. In most situations, it is considered *bearish* (i.e., a sign that the stock price is likely to fall) in the case of insider selling and is considered *bullish* (i.e., a sign that the stock price is likely to rise) in the case of insider buying. After all, insiders have the greatest knowledge about the company.

That's really an oversimplification of insider buying and selling. In actuality, on average, corporate insiders are *net sellers;* they sell two to three shares for every one share they buy. Thus, when insiders are buying or *holding onto* their stock, they place a high priority on rewarding shareholders (including themselves), thereby managing for the long term.

Insider selling—especially if the insiders are not selling a majority of their shares—should not necessarily be considered alarming.

There are numerous reasons to sell stock—to buy a house, to pay for college tuition, to pay off a debt, and so forth. Also, it is often seen as a reward for "hanging on there" so long. Consequently, the older the insiders who are selling their stock, the less the concern. However, if insider selling is *excessive,* or if insider selling is implemented by fairly young managers, then investors should think twice before investing.

Be Cautious of Selling Shareholders

In the case of IPOs, there is generally no insider buying; insiders are either holding onto their stock or *cashing out.*

Does it matter whether the proceeds from an initial public offering go to the selling shareholders or to the company? The important issue is what *percentage* of a shareholder's stock is being sold. If most of the proceeds from an offering go to selling shareholders and not to fuel a company's growth, it often conveys a message that the insiders who are selling their shares lack confidence that the company will be a strong performer in the future. When Vector Graphic went public, for example, half of the proceeds went to the selling shareholders, rather than to Vector Graphic itself. This reinforced the other turnoffs identified earlier associated with Vector Graphic.

Like Vector Graphic, when Atlantic Research Corporation went public, only half the proceeds went to the company. Moreover, the two top executives at Atlantic Research—President Coleman Raphael (now business school dean at George Mason University) and Vice-President Borten—sold 25% of their stock at that time. Likewise, their largest outside investor also sold 25% of its stock. Despite this, Atlantic Research performed rather well in subsequent years. Insiders at Maxicare and Worlds of Wonder also sold substantial amounts of their stock holdings at the time they went public; these companies, however, did not perform nearly as well as Atlantic Research. In contrast, at Compaq Computer the existing shareholders kept all their shares when the company went public. Compaq's subsequent performance was outstanding. Thus, as noted, insider selling (or lack thereof) is just *one* indicator of a company's aftermarket performance. It becomes more meaningful in light of the other turnons and turnoffs noted earlier.

An interesting example involving selling shareholders occurred at Microsoft. First, let's take a look at the selling shareholders and try to gauge whether the amounts were excessive. CEO Gates, who owned over 49% of the stock, totaling over 11 million shares (which incidentally were worth over $235 million at the offering date and are now worth over $2 billion), planned to sell only 80,000 shares (not even 1% of his holdings at the time of the IPO). The only "large" seller at Microsoft (a decision the company probably regrets today) was the venture capital firm Technology Venture Investors (TVI) which sold 21% of its stock. (Nonetheless, TVI did exceedingly well on its early stage investment in Microsoft.) Also, Bill Gates' parents, apparently not as adventurous as their son, sold 29% of their holdings. Who ever said "father knows best?"

The original offering of Microsoft was only for 2.8 million shares, roughly 11% of the company. We suppose that CEO Bill Gates and other shareholders wanted to keep as much of a good thing for themselves as possible.

PRIOR FUNDING

Look for Companies That Have Already Received Substantial Funding, Especially from Venture Capitalists

Many early stage companies struggle for two main reasons— lack of funding and lack of good advice and direction. In some cases, a company could alleviate both these concerns by getting the backing of a solid group of venture capitalists. Not only do these early stage ventures receive an infusion of much needed capital—equally important—they receive the benefit of the wisdom and experience of venture capitalists. Apple Computer, for example, was one such beneficiary when Venrock Associates invested in the fledgling company.

We have found that the active support, involvement, and investment by established venture capital firms (or venture capital subsidiaries of large corporations) is a very strong predictor of the success or failure of an emerging growth company. This is especially true for high-tech firms, which often need $10 to $50 million of private funding at early stages of their development. For example, Genentech benefited financially when The Lubrizol Corporation contributed $10 million in exchange for 24% of the stock of the company. In addition, the venture capital firm Kleiner Perkins not only invested a sizable amount in this early stage company, but also was responsible for providing Genentech with its CEO, Robert Swanson, who is still running the company today. Of course, in addition to Genentech benefiting, so have Lubrizol and Kleiner Perkins benefited from their relationship with Genentech, as evidenced by the remarkable increase in the value of their investment.

ACTIVE SUPPORT, INVOLVEMENT, AND IN-VESTMENT BY ESTABLISHED VENTURE CAPI-TAL FIRMS IS A VERY STRONG PREDICTOR OF THE SUCCESS OF AN EMERGING GROWTH COMPANY.

Significant early stage investments from venture investors have benefited a number of retailers, as well. For example, Costco received early financing from the French manufacturing company, Carrefour, in the form of $30 million of debt and equity. By contrast, Home Shopping Network was financed internally with about $120,000 it paid in capital and had debt of about $16 million in short-term and long-term obligations—that's far from ideal—at the time of its offering. HSN clearly lacked the benefits of an association with any established venture capital firms.

Be Wary of Companies That Have Been Turned Down for Funding

Not surprisingly, ZZZZ Best had significant difficulty in obtaining prior funding. As stated in its prospectus:

> Due to various factors, including the rapidity of its growth, the limited amount of its liquid assets and the absence of any fixed assets ... capable of serving as collateral for a loan, the Company has been unable, on its own, to obtain financing from traditional lending sources.

Thus, ZZZZ Best, which was going public as its only means of raising capital, never received the advice that generally accompanies a relationship with venture capitalists.

VALUATION

Traditional Ways to Value Established Companies

The traditional way to value a company is generally based on its past performance, as reflected in its financial statements. There is usually a recognizable relationship between a company's stock price and its earnings, revenues, cash flows, and assets.

In the previous chapter, we discussed the use of the P–E (or price-earnings) ratio of a stock as a measure of the company's value. P–E's are critical because, as indicated earlier, *over the long term*, the value of a company is driven by earnings.

The P–E ratio (or the P–E multiple, or simply, the *multiple*) is the relationship between the stock price and the earnings of the company. In other words, if a company selling at $10 a share has 1 million shares outstanding, and earns (i.e., its NIAT) $1 million—or $1 per share— then its P–E would be:

$$\underset{\text{(price)}}{\$10 \text{ per share}} \,/\, \underset{\text{(earnings)}}{\$1 \text{ per share}} = 10$$

The P–E is a closely-watched number that is found in the daily stock tables of any major newspaper. For example, on January 22, 1991, we found the following information for Compaq Computer Corp., whose P–E ratio was 14 on that day:

52 wks			Yld	P–E	Sales				Net
Hi	Lo	Stock	Divid %	Ratio	100s	Hi	Low	Close	Chg
67	35	Compaq		14	10279	63	61 1/2	62 1/2	-1/8

The P–E ratio can be a useful measure for determining whether a stock is overpriced, underpriced, or fairly priced, relative to other similar companies. Obviously, because the P–E ratio is based on earnings, it becomes more meaningful as earnings become more predictable. P–Es are also a measure of volatility. The higher the P–E, the higher the potential return, as well as risk. This is common for emerging growth companies.

P-ES ARE A MEASURE OF VOLATILITY. THE HIGHER THE P-E, THE HIGHER THE POTENTIAL RETURN, AS WELL AS RISKS.

If a company is selling at a P–E of 10 (i.e., 10 times its earnings), it may be fairly valued relative to its industry. In *bull markets* (i.e., when stock prices are rising), P–E ratios tend to be higher; so, it is quite common to see P–E ratios of 15-20 for established companies. For the darlings of Wall Street—which have recently included such outstanding blue chip companies as Merck, Gillette, Johnson & Johnson, Procter & Gamble, and PepsiCo—it is common to see P–E's of 20–25 during bull (upwardly moving) markets. The more volatile growth companies command even higher premiums during upswings in the market. If we go back about 20 years, we see that some of the blue chip companies of today were hot growth companies of the early 1970s. In 1972, for example, Digital Equipment Corporation (DEC) commanded a P–E multiple of 80 and Disney had a P–E of 78. IBM seemed relatively *underpriced* at that time with a P–E of only 41.

A P–E ratio also measures how long it would take to recover your investment, assuming that earnings *stayed the same*. For example, if IBM's P–E were at 10 currently, then it would take 10 years for an investor to make back his or her investment, assuming that earnings stayed *constant*.

Thus, the higher the P–E, the more pressure is on the company to increase its earnings in order to make it a sensible investment. In 1972, McDonald's was selling at $75 a share, or a P–E of about 50. As good a company as McDonald's was—and is—it could not live up to its expectation of earnings growth, and soon fell to $25 a share, thereby resulting in a more realistic P–E. Similarly, Polaroid had a P–E of 50 when its stock hit $143 in 1973. Within a year and a half, the stock price dropped to $14.

More extreme in terms of P–E ratios was Electronic Data System's (EDS) P–E of 500 in 1969. That would mean that if earnings remained constant, it would take 500 years for an investor to make back his or her investment. Like McDonald's, EDS was, and still is (although it is now owned by General Motors) an outstanding company. However, despite a dramatic *increase* in sales and earnings, the stock price actually *declined* from $40 to $3 in 1974, due to its overpriced condition. Similar to EDS, Polaroid's stock tumbled from $74 in mid-1972 to $8 in 1974. Thus, it should be clear that high P–Es are associated with high volatility.

One more issue regarding P–Es as they relate to investments. The investor cannot just rely on the absolute value of the P–E when making an investment decision. P–Es are important in comparison to other similar companies in similar industries at similar times. So Microsoft, for example, can be a real bargain at a P–E of 15 (which is somewhat comparable to its competitors), whereas a utility company such as American Electric Power can be exceedingly overpriced at a P–E of 10 (when other utilities have a P–E of 5 to 8).

Valuation for IPOs

For IPOs, P–Es can often be 40, 60, 80, or even 100 or more times earnings, since such companies may not have a consistent earnings pattern. Moreover, the P–Es for IPOs will often be meaningless, since many of these companies have "been in the red" (i.e., they have not shown a profit) throughout their history. In many such instances, therefore, valuations based on a *multiple of revenues*, rather than based on a multiple of earnings, becomes a somewhat better indicator of a company's "value."

When it comes to IPOs, traditional measures of valuation—such as P–Es—make the most sense for those new issues *with a sufficiently long track record*. For example, Liz Claiborne had a history of rapid sales growth and steady profitability since its inception in 1976. For the year just prior to going public, 1980, its sales totaled $79 million and its net income totaled $6.2 million. When comparing the IPO market valuation—i.e., the total number of shares outstanding times the proposed IPO price per share of stock—of $66 million to its most recent sales of $79 million (which incidentally had increased by 243% over the previous two years prior to its IPO) the multiple of market price to sales was less than 1.0. Likewise, at the IPO per share price of $19, the P–E multiple was less than 10. Similarly, Federal Express, a six-year old company at the time of its IPO, was valued at $81 million at its offering, a modest valuation of only 10 times its most recent earnings and only 74% of its sales revenues. Those were indeed conservative multiples for these profitable high-growth companies. Their subsequent appreciation in stock price confirmed that Liz

Claiborne and Federal Express were attractive buys at those valuations.

When analyzing the attractiveness of investments in emerging growth companies, we chart out their market valuations, *both* as a multiple of *revenues* and of *earnings*, to provide an indication of how fairly they are valued. This is information that is easy to obtain from the financial statements of a prospectus.

Valuing High Flyers Requires More Creativity

In valuing an emerging growth company with a limited history and rapidly changing financial results, traditional valuation techniques are often insufficient. The valuation of these "high flyers," in large part, is based on *expectations* of future growth. As such, the investor needs to ask whether those expectations underlying the valuation appear to be reasonable. If the company becomes a "star," then what may *appear* to be a high valuation might not turn out to be so.

For Apple, whose earnings had grown by 700% in the three years immediately prior to its IPO in 1980, underwriter Morgan Stanley was able to price the stock at a premium over similar high-tech gowth companies such as Tandem, Paradyne, ROLM, and so forth—which had gone public earlier. Specifically, those high-tech companies were selling at approximately 18 times *anticipated* earnings. Apple, despite already phenomenal earnings growth, was priced at nearly 100 times its most recent year's earnings. (The company had earned $11.7 million and had a market valuation at the time of its IPO in excess of $1 billion.) This translated into extremely attractive returns for the early stage private investors as well as the founders of the company. Arthur Rock's $57,600 investment in 1977 grew to $14 million in 3 years. Steven Jobs did quite well for himself as well; his shares were worth $165 million at the time of the IPO. Nonetheless, for a company with so much promise, such a high valuation did not seem out of line. Investors that recognized this fared extremely well.

For the investors who missed out on Apple when it went public, they had another outstanding opportunity when Compaq went public in 1983 in a $100 million offering. Although Compaq had been in operation for only 9 months, it was valued at over $400 million or 5 times its annualized revenues. Clearly, its valuation was based on the expectation that revenues would grow by several fold over the next few years. Although the valuation may have seemed high, it sustained its remarkable growth over the ensuing years, thereby enabling its market value to increase by 8-fold since it went public.

Turning away from high-tech companies, the IPO market valuation of Reebok—at $260 million—seemed high, relative to its most recent year's revenues and earnings: 4 times revenues and 43 times earnings. However, based on the annualized revenues and earnings for the year in which Reebok was going public (using only 4 months of operations), the valuation would translate into less than 2 times revenues and only 14 times earnings. In other words, the company was quite fairly valued as long as revenues and earnings would continue to grow at its prior rate.

Not All Fast-Growth, High-Tech Companies Have Excessive Valuations

Of course, some high-tech growth companies have a conservative valuation. Microsoft was valued at $519 million at its offering in 1986, which was a fairly conservative 22 times earnings, considering the high-flying nature of the overall stock market at that time. It was reasonable to assume that, given all the positive characteristics of the company identified earlier, there was room for significant appreciation in its stock price following its IPO. The shrewd investors who bought Microsoft at the time of its IPO realized a 9-fold increase in their investment in just four years.

Watch Out for Those Companies with Outrageous Valuations

But there's always ZZZZ Best to demonstrate how new issues can be overvalued. It had generated sales of approximately $4.8 million in the year immediately prior to its IPO. Yet, the company's market valuation was $44 million—or 9 times revenues and nearly 50 times earnings.

EQUITY ARRANGEMENT

The prospectus clearly delineates the relative investment made by the existing and new investors in the company. Generally, this is laid out neatly in such a chart as follows:

	Shares Purchased #(000) %	Consideration Amt ($000) %	Avg Price/ Share
Existing Investors			
New Investors			
TOTAL			

Such a chart will highlight whether the financial arrangement is "equitable" for the new investors.

Look for Substantial Investments Made by Existing Shareholders

We like to see an equitable financial arrangement for the new investors, in which the existing shareholders have made a financial investment in the business. This is evident in the case of Costco. The existing stockholders had invested over $33 million, or 51% of the total consideration. In the case of Sun Microsystems, the existing shareholders contributed over $40 million, or 46% of the total consideration. This shows a sharing of risk by new and existing investors.

We are often concerned when the existing shareholders—particularly the management team—of a company have invested little or none of their own money in a business. Take the case of Jan Bell Marketing, which went public in August 1987. Entrepreneur Alan Lipton and his management team were offering 20% of the company in exchange for $13 million—while Lipton et al. retained 80% of the equity while having invested only $277,000. As we said earlier, however, we can't overrely on just one or two predictors of success. As it turned out, Jan Bell became almost an immediate superstar performer over its first three years as a public company, despite its seemingly inequitable financial arrangement. More recently, its stock lost 80% of its value from its highest levels. Similarly, the existing shareholder of TCBY (there was only one—Frank D. Hickingbotham) contributed only $88,800, representing 3.6% of the total contribution, while retaining 71% of the company. Although the new shareholders contributed over 96% of the capital, they had virtually no control of the company. Like Jan Bell, TCBY was an early success story on Wall Street, increasing in stock value by 30-fold in six years. More recently, the stock has lost more than 80% of its value.

> *WE ARE CONCERNED WHEN THE EXISTING SHAREHOLDERS OF A COMPANY HAVE INVESTED LITTLE OR NONE OF THEIR OWN MONEY IN A BUSINESS.*

More extreme is the case of Home Shopping Network (HSN). At the IPO, the company collected a total of $28,851,500 from the sale of stock. Of that total, the new shareholders contributed $28,800,000 (or 99.8% of the total) for just 11.6% of the stock. The existing shareholders, who had contributed only $51,500 (or 0.2% of the total) owned 88.4% of the company. It seemed to us that the existing shareholders had risked very little of their own resources.

It is not surprising that the three companies just mentioned—Jan Bell, TCBY, and HSN—have had some of the "rockiest rides" among recent IPOs. Although each gained in value initially, they each subsequently lost most of their value from their highest levels.

Look to the Prospectus for Answers

Fortunately, as noted earlier, the prospectus lays out very carefully the amount invested by existing and new shareholders and their relative ownership of the company. For example, the prospectus of Vector Graphic clearly displayed the inequitable deal for the new shareholders. The existing shareholders had very little of their own money at risk. As shown by the chart below, the new (i.e., public) investors in Vector Graphic were paying almost 80 times the purchase price per share paid by the existing stockholders. Yet, although the new investors invested nearly 90% of the capital, they only owned 9% of the company.

VECTOR GRAPHIC

	Shares Purchased # (000)	%	Consideration Amt ($000)	%	Avg Price/ Share
Existing Investors	5,125	91%	$852	12%	$ 0.17
New Investors	500	9%	$6,500	88%	$13.00
TOTAL	5,625	100%	$7,352	100%	

Similarly, there's ZZZZ Best, which was certainly far from "z best" deal for "z investor" as demonstrated below:

	Shares Purchased # (000)	%	Consideration Amt ($000)	%	Avg Price/ Share
Existing Investors	7,778	70%	$ 1,239	9%	$ 0.16
New Investors	3,300	30%	$13,200	91%	$ 4.00
TOTAL	11,078	100%	$14,439	100%	

Vector Graphic and ZZZZ Best were certainly far from outstanding performers. However, despite an inequitable financial arrangement, some companies still become star performers. For example, despite the somewhat inequitable situation for the new shareholders of Reebok (as outlined in the following chart which was contained in Reebok's prospectus), new investors still earned handsome returns.

	Shares Purchased		Consideration		Avg Price/ Share
	# (000)	%	Amt ($000)	%	
Existing Investors	13,315	87%	$1,619	4%	$ 0.12
New Investors	2,000	13%	$34,000	96%	$13.00
TOTAL	15,315	100%	$35,619	100%	

As shown above, the existing owners retained nearly 90% of the company for a $1.6 million investment, whereas the new investors, who invested $34 million, owned only 13% of the company. Despite this inequity, there were enough positive factors working for Reebok to enable the company to appreciate over its early years as a public company. It has since declined in value somewhat.

QUALITY OF UNDERWRITER

Over the short term, just about any underwriter can take a company public and hype it up enough to prompt an immediate increase in the price of its stock. However, over the long term, quality will win out. We have found that the "quality companies" tend to be underwritten by the "quality underwriters."

By quality, we're generally referring to the more recognizable underwriters that have strong research departments and are selective about the companies that they choose to take public. That would include such underwriters as Goldman Sachs, First Boston, Bear Stearns, Merrill Lynch, Morgan Stanley, Alex Brown, Hambrecht & Quist, Piper Jaffray Hopwood, Donaldson Lufkin Jenrette (DLJ), and so forth. Certainly, each of these underwriters has had its share of "losers." However, each has had numerous individual successes (for example, Goldman Sachs underwrote Microsoft; Bear Stearns underwrote Home Depot; Merrill Lynch underwrote Liz Claiborne; Hambrecht & Quist underwrote Adobe Systems; Morgan Stanley underwrote Apple), but, more important, each has had a strong *overall* track record when it comes to IPOs.

The Best and the Worst

A casual glance of the best performing and worst performing underwriters of new issues *over the long term* shows a stark contrast between the two groups. Based on a recent study reported in *Forbes* magazine, the leading underwriters over the 1980s in terms of average post-IPO performance of companies that they've underwritten were:[1]

Underwriter	# of issues	% of issues: that increased	that beat market	Avg. performance: over-all	relative to market
Piper Jaffray	26 %	65 %	96 %	115.9 %	43.7 %
Bear Stearns	57	21	91	148.0	27.3
First Boston	54	54	93	56.5	16.6
Goldman Sachs	85	64	94	64.8	10.9
William Blair	36	58	83	68.5	4.6
DLJ	72	43	93	49.2	1.7

The worst performers were certainly not household names:

Underwriter	# of issues	% of issues: that increased	that beat market	Avg. performance: over-all	relative to market
Rotan Mosle	21 %	24 %	86 %	-48.2 %	-67.3 %
Rauscher Pierce Refsnes	17	29	94	-26.8	-47.4
Bateman Eichler	18	33	83	-24.5	-47.3
Dain Bosworth	22	36	91	-2.0	-42.0
Ladenberg Thalman	25	28	92	1.9	-40.3
Becker Paribas	24	50	96	27.1	-37.8

---

[1] See *Forbes*, June 25, 1990, pgs. 273–274.

Several of the lesser-known underwriters have been responsible for underwriting a large percentage of failing companies. The underwriters with the greatest percentage of bankruptcies during the 1980s are as follows:

Muller (83.3%)

Rooney Pace (36.4%)

J Muir (33.3%)

DH Blair (30.8%)

Howard Weill Labouisse (22.2%)

Not surprisingly, Muller, Rooney Pace, and J Muir are no longer in business.

Of course, some of the smaller, lesser-known underwriters have had high performing new issues. For example, Federal Express, which had increased in value by 25-fold up until the crash of 1987, was underwritten by White Weld & Co, hardly a big name underwriter. Moreover, some of the larger, established underwriters have had winners *and* losers. For example, Merrill Lynch underwrote Liz Claiborne and Home Shopping Network. However, we have found that new issues underwritten by the "quality" underwriters have, on balance, far outperformed those of the lesser-regarded underwriters over the long term.

FINANCIAL ARRANGEMENT: SUMMARY POINTS

- Search for companies that use the proceeds from an offering to foster future growth
- Be cautious when funding is targeted for working capital
- Beware of companies which use funding to repay debt ...
- ...But, in some cases, using the proceeds to reduce debt is desirable
- Be cautious of selling shareholders
- Look for companies that have already received substantial funding, especially from established venture capitalists
- Be wary of companies that were previously turned down for funding
- Valuing high flyers requires more creativity
- Not all fast-growth, high-tech companies have excessive valuations
- Watch out for those companies with outrageous valuations
- Look for substantial investments made by existing shareholders
- Consider the quality of the underwriter

PART THREE

Tomorrow's Winners and Losers

CHAPTER 8

Identifying the Companies

APPLYING OUR FRAMEWORK TO THE WINNERS AND LOSERS OF TOMORROW

We already know what happened to Compaq, Lotus, ZZZZ Best, and so forth. Up to this point, this book has used a new framework in examining the performance of emerging growth companies over the last fifteen years. We demonstrated our approach on companies for which we already knew how they performed. Our purpose was to describe a framework with the use of illustrations from well-known emerging growth companies over the last fifteen years.

Now, we are ready to apply our framework to current emerging growth companies and to predict (hopefully with some degree of accuracy) the winners and losers of the nineties. We have examined the prospectuses of companies that have recently filed registration statements for a public offering and were (at the time this book was written) in the process of going public (or had recently gone public). The time frame is from the end of 1989 through the middle of 1990.

We examined the companies in an attempt to determine which predictive factors—both turnons and turnoffs—were present.

OUR SAMPLE

Out of the more than 100 registrations taking place during the time period, we have selected *ten* companies that we feel are representative of the IPOs of the time. The companies range from early stage to well-established ventures; they range from those having a partial management team to those having an experienced and capable management team with a solid group of directors; they range from a situation in which none of the existing shareholders sell shares of stock in the company to a situation in which there is a significant sell off of equity by the existing shareholders, and so forth.

The ten companies, arranged alphabetically, are as follows:

Company	*Stock Symbol*	*Proposed IPO Price*
Brooksfilms	BKS	10
Cellular Information Systems	CALLA	10 3/4
Cisco Systems	CSCO	15 1/2
Digital Sound Corp.	DGSD	7 1/4
Integrated Systems	INTS	6 3/4
Orbital Sciences	ORBI	15
Readers Digest Association	RDA	20
Safeway Stores	SWY	15
Sullivan Dental Products	SULL	9 1/4
Xenejenex	XNJX	5

A brief description of each of the above named companies follows:

Brooksfilms develops, produces, and distributes overseas feature-length motion pictures and television programming. Mel Brooks (the entertainer) serves as the chairman and CEO. Over the past 20 years, the company, together with Mr. Brooks, has produced, coproduced, or been involved in the creation of 18 motion picture features. The company's strategy is to continue to produce quality motion pictures that are distributed domestically by major theatrical motion picture distributors while retaining foreign rights for the company. The company intends to expand its operations by acquiring foreign distribution rights to motion pictures produced by others and by retaining foreign distribution rights.

Cellular Information Systems is a cellular communications company that operates cellular telephone systems and owns controlling interests in cellular systems serving 13 Metropolitan Statistical Areas (MSAs). Cellular also owns options or has agreements to acquire interests in systems serving other MSAs or Rural Service Areas (RSAs). As of November, 1989, there were nearly 7,000 total subscribers for the operating cellular telephone systems in which the company owned interest. The company was in the developmental stage prior to 1988, during which time its activities were concentrated on the acquisition of controlling interests in cellular authorizations and construction and initial operation of cellular systems. Thus, there are only two years of operating history in which to base an analysis.

Cisco Systems, a 5-year old company, develops, manufactures, markets, and supports high performance, multiprotocol internetworking systems that enable its customers to build large-scale, integrated computer networks. Its principal products support more protocols than any competing vendor, providing the user with quality and efficiency advantages made possible from Cisco's proprietary software technology. The technology is an outgrowth of efforts at Stanford University to integrate computers of several manufacturers into an integrated "network of networks." Although Cisco has been selling its products for less than three years (its first two years were devoted primarily to research and development), the company, through its direct sales force and manufacturer reps, has installed over 4,000 systems for more than 400 customers throughout the world. Its customer list includes: computer systems vendors (such as IBM, DEC, H–P); industrial corporations (AT&T, Ford, GE, Xerox); financial companies (Aetna, Morgan Stanley); universities (Stanford, Harvard, MIT, Princeton); international corporations (Matsushita, Siemens); and the U. S. government.

Digital Sound Corporation designs, manufactures, and markets general purpose hardware and software that can operate multiple voice processing applications simultaneously. These applications include voice messaging, voice mail, speech recognition, and so forth. Digital was incorporated in 1977, but actually began selling its current set of applications in 1985. The company has installed over 800 systems in the U.S., Canada, and Europe.

Integrated Systems Inc. designs, develops, markets, and supports an integrated family of CAE/CASE software products that automate and accelerate the development of real-time software and systems. Its products, used in the aerospace, automotive, industrial automation, and computer peripherals industries, provide users with advantages in terms of time, cost, performance, functionality, and reliability for real-time software and system development. Integrated believes that it is one of the first companies to offer development tools that combine CAE and CASE technologies specifically for use by real-time systems engineers.

Orbital Sciences Corporation, launched in 1982, is a space technology company that designs, develops, and markets space products and services such as space transportation systems (e.g., space and suborbital launch vehicles), space support systems (e.g., satellite tracking systems), and satellite systems (e.g., spacecraft platforms). In 1988, Orbital acquired Space Data Corporation, which has enabled Orbital to expand its product lines. Orbital sells its products to government and university customers.

Reader's Digest *Association* (RDA) is an international publisher and direct mail marketer of magazines, books, recorded music, and other products. The company has been the publisher of *Reader's Digest* magazine, which has a worldwide circulation of 28 million, since 1922. The company's other products include *Reader's Digest Condensed Books,* special interest magazines, and home entertainment products.

Safeway Stores, founded in 1926, is one of the largest food retailers in the world. Currently, the company operates more than 1,100 stores in the United States and Canada. In 1986, Safeway, then a publicly held corporation, was acquired in a leveraged buyout (LBO) by a corporation formed by the investment firm Kohlberg Kravis Roberts & Co. (KKR). Since the LBO, Safeway has restructured its operations and has sold off $2.4 billion worth of assets, thereby reducing its debt from $5.8 billion at the time of the LBO to $3.1 billion at the end of 1989.

Sullivan Dental Products, founded in 1980, is a distributor of dental equipment and dental supplies. The company markets products through its direct sales force and by a catalog which features over 7,000 items. The company is planning to open a distribution center on the West Coast to attract new customers and to speed up delivery time to customers in that region of the country.

Xenejenex Inc., a developmental stage company, creates, produces, and distributes health care videotapes. The company has created and produced three videotapes to date: *Feeling Good With Arthritis* featuring Mickey Mantle; *Radon Free* featuring Dick Van Patten; and *Coming of Age: A Video Guide to Healthy Aging* featuring Eddie Albert. The company financed the production of the first two videotapes through limited partnerships; the other videotape was paid for by Marion Laboratories. Xenejenex currently distributes these videotapes through videostores and catalogs. The company has also developed a free lending library program, *America's Hottest Health Care Videos*, that will be sold to retail establishments and to corporate sponsors. Its first corporate sponsor is Pfizer.

WINNERS, LOSERS, AND ANYTHING IN BETWEEN

Of the ten companies listed above, we find three categories, based on the predictive factors cited throughout the book. These categories, which take into account risk/return profiles, are as follows:

- Clear *winners*
  - Cisco Systems
  - Integrated Systems
  - *Reader's Digest* Association
  - Sullivan Dental Products
- *Bumpy rides*
  - Orbital Science
  - Safeway Stores
- Clear *losers*
  - Brooksfilms
  - Cellular Information Systems
  - Digital Sound
  - Xenejenex

It is important to note that both risk and return enter into our evaluations. Thus, our lower rated companies may become high fliers, at least over the short term. However, like Home Shopping Network, Silk Greenhouse, and the like, we feel that they may be highly susceptible to rapid and significant declines in their stock price. Similarly, our higher rated companies might not be the *best* performers of the bunch. However, we feel that there is ample room for stock appreciation, with limited downside risk.

A LOOK AHEAD

The next three chapters parallel the three categories above. In those chapters, we'll examine the ten companies mentioned above in greater detail, and will apply our framework to them as a means of assessing their investment potential.

CHAPTER 9

The "Winners"

- **Cisco Systems**
- **Integrated Systems**
- ***Reader's Digest* Association**
- **Sullivan Dental Products**

Throughout this book, we've differentiated between the "winners" and "losers" based on a number of predictive factors. One important distinctive feature of these two groups is the relative risk of the investment. There is substantially less risk associated with the "winners" as compared to the "losers." Thus, the "winners" should not be viewed as "can't miss opportunities;" rather, the risk/return trade-off appears *more* attractive for such investments. Similarly, the risk/return trade-off for the "losers" appears *less* attractive.

Of the ten companies that we've categorized, we rate four of them as "winners:"

- Cisco Systems
- Integrated Systems
- *Reader's Digest* Association (RDA)
- Sullivan Dental Products

Cisco Systems and Integrated Systems are two high-tech companies with tremendous potential, yet with limited downside risks. *Reader's Digest* Association and Sullivan are successful, established companies that are expected to provide above average returns to investors, while having virtually none of the risks associated with early stage, emerging growth companies. Thus, we expect that these four companies will provide superior risk adjusted returns for investors.

CISCO SYSTEMS

I. Product/Market

Turnons: Cisco's products were designed specifically to interconnect multiple heterogeneous networks into a single integrated network, to support significantly more interfaces and protocols than any other supplier and to offer a high level of network intelligence through the company's dynamic routing software technology. Thus, Cisco, although a fairly new business, has significant competitive advantages in terms of the benefits that its proprietary (although not yet patented) products provide for its users.

It is unclear what the state of competition will be over the coming years. Of course, the giants of the computer industry may play a significant role in this industry in the years to come. However, several of them—including IBM and DEC—are already customers of Cisco, and may not make their presence a factor in this focused segment of the workstation industry.

Turnoffs: We have some concerns about competition and developments in this industry. The market for internetworking systems, such as the ones designed and manufactured by Cisco, has the potential to become highly competitive and subject to rapid technological change.

II. Management and Organization

Turnons: Cisco has assembled a talented and diverse group of executives to foster the continued growth of the company. The top managers have experience with such outstanding companies as IBM, Hewlett Packard, Digital Equipment, and AT&T (which, presumably, by no strange coincidence, have become customers of Cisco), and will likely facilitate future business contacts. Moreover, there is an excellent mix of skills in engineering, marketing, finance, and general management.

The academic credentials of the top level managers are excellent; combined, they hold *seven* degrees in business and/or engineering from Stanford, not to mention a few more from such other prestigious schools as Harvard, University of Pennsylvania, Cambridge, and so forth. Thus, it should not be surprising that the company, founded by two directors of computer facilities at Stanford, has been able to attract such customers as Stanford, Harvard, Princeton, MIT, University of Chicago, University of Pennsylvania, University of Texas, and several other universities, which are prime customers for Cisco's products.

Cisco has also assembled a talented group of outside directors for the company, which came from the venture capital industry—for example, Don Valentine (a founder of National Semiconductor, and, later, of the venture capital firm Sequoia Capital), who has been involved in the early growth of Apple Computer, Atari, LSI Logic, Sierra Semiconductor, and several other Silicon Valley companies.

Turnoffs: Executives who have been with the company for a very short time have been granted sizeable stock options. For example, John Morgridge, who joined the company as president and CEO in October, 1988, was granted options to purchase 755,000 shares of stock over a 4-year period at $.03 per share. That $25,000 investment is equal to about $12 million, based on the proposed offering price.

III. Financial Position

(Note: Revenue and income are reported in $000)			
	1987	1988	1989	*% change '88–'89*
Revenues	1,485	5,450	27,664	408%
Gross Profit	664	3,005	16,002	433%
Oper. Income	130	555	6,758	1118%
NIAT	83	388	4,178	977%

Turnons: Cisco's revenues have increased by nearly 20-fold to $28 million in the 2-year period from fiscal year 1987 through 1989. Based on the first quarter's results (revenues of $14 million), the company is on target to more than double its revenues for 1990.

Even more impressive than its high growth is the company's profitability. Cisco has been profitable since it began selling its products and has posted higher margins over the past few years.

Gross profits have increased by 24-fold from 1987 to 1989, with gross margins in the exceedingly attractive range of 60%. In fact, in the first quarter of the 1990 fiscal year, gross margins were at 63%. Over the past year, operating margins have been around 24% and net profit margins have been approximately 15%.

Cisco has been a very attractive performer for its investors thus far; in 1989, its return on assets was 25% and its return on equity was 56%.

Long term debt, which is currently about $300,000, is quite low for a company that is generating over $30 million in revenues. Total debt is currently approximately 50% of total assets.

Turnoffs: Cisco has been realizing higher levels of profitability as a result of economies of scale from increased volumes of sales, which are on an upward trend as of now. However, the company states in its prospectus that its expansion efforts are likely to result in lower levels of profits, at least over the short term.

R & D as a percentage of revenues has declined from about 14% in 1987 and 1988 to less than 8% in 1989. Often, percentage declines in R & D are indicative of a short term focus; however, in the case of Cisco, it is probably more indicative of significant increases in revenues, that have just happened to outpace expenditures on R & D. Nonetheless, this expense should be monitored. It should be considered a red flag if R & D expenditures as a percentage of revenues declines significantly over the next year or two.

In examining Cisco's balance sheet, we find that accounts receivable increased by 8-fold, or twice the rate of the company's revenues, to $7.5 million.

IV. Financial Arrangement

| | Shares Purchased | | Consideration | | Avg Price/ |
	# (000)	%	Amt ($000)	%	Share
Existing Investors	10,117	81%	$2,805	7%	$0.28
New Investors	2,390	19%	$37,045	93%	$15.50
TOTAL	12,507	100%	$39,850	100%	

Turnons: A positive factor for Cisco is that it has been able to raise a significant amount of early stage funding, principally from Sequoia Capital.

The existing large shareholders will be retaining their stock, presumably because they feel that there is significant upside potential for such an investment. The largest shareholder, Sequoia Capital, which is the venture capital firm managed by Don Valentine (who is one of the most knowledgeable venture capitalists in this country), will retain its entire equity stake, which is nearly one-fourth of the outstanding stock of the company. This is an excellent indicator of a sophisticated investor's strong confidence in the investment value of a company. After all, if Don Valentine, who is chairman of the board of Cisco, and is, therefore, as knowledgeable as anyone on the company's developments and outlook, feels that Cisco is a good investment at the time of its IPO, then the public investors may wish to follow his lead.

Using annualized revenues and income for 1990, Cisco's valuation would be approximately 3 1/2 times revenues, 12 times operating income, and 19 times net income, which are *reasonable* for such a company. As such, although it may still take a few years for the company's revenues and earnings to reflect its true value, even at a valuation of $194 million, or $15.50 per share, there is an opportunity for significant appreciation in the stock value of the company.

Turnoffs: Cisco seems to be financing its short term needs—i.e., receivables and inventory—with long term financing. A potential problem that we see is that as inventory levels rise too rapidly, it may force the company to sell off any oversupplies of inventory at discounted prices, thereby depressing margins. This is important particularly in high-tech companies subject to rapid technological change (such as Cisco), that are more likely to be "stuck" with obsolete inventory.

Overall Analysis

Cisco has very attractive product/market opportunities. Although there are significant obstacles due to the competitive nature of the industry and rapidly changing technology, Cisco has developed an attractive customer base and has assembled an experienced, diverse group of managers who have played key roles in the growth of similar high tech ventures in the past.

We have a concern about the high valuation of the company and feel that it could take a few years for the company to realize its potential. However, experienced, sophisticated investors like Don Valentine of Sequoia are confident enough of Cisco's future to retain their ownership stakes in the company. This has strong implications for the public investors who now have an opportunity to invest in Cisco as well.

Very often, high-tech companies like Cisco can perform extremely well right at the time of their IPOs, especially if high-tech stocks are doing well at the time. This could mean a 20% or higher return in a matter of weeks or months, despite the relatively high valuation of the company at its present price. This, however, is just the nature of high-tech growth oriented IPO's with excellent *potential.* And, just as there is substantial upside for a company like Cisco, there is the possibility for a dramatic downside movement in the price of the stock, especially if technology stocks go "out of favor." In any case, Cisco may be a rather volatile performer in the near future.

More important, however, is the long-term potential of the company. Cisco appears to be a very attractive *long-term* investment opportunity (as well as a potential short-term success), provided that the company can sustain its revenues and earnings growth over the coming years.

In summary, Cisco has strong fundamentals and, despite a somewhat high offering valuation, it may appreciate significantly immediately following its IPO. Of course, such technology companies, no matter how solid, are volatile, thereby making Cisco susceptible to price declines if the stock market as a whole (and technology stocks especially) performs poorly. Nonetheless, the long-term outlook for this well-managed company appears very solid. We feel that Cisco has the potential to be one of the better performing high-tech stocks over the coming years.

INTEGRATED SYSTEMS

I. Product/Market

Turnons: Integrated has the competitive advantage of a proprietary software technology, and is protected to some extent via copyright, trademark, patent, contract, and so forth.

Turnoffs: Integrated's revenues are derived largely from companies in the automotive, aerospace, and defense industries. These are cyclical industries that may impact heavily on the variation in sales for Integrated over the coming years. Integrated is dependent upon the cyclicality of these industries and upon selected customers for its revenue growth.

II. Management and Organization

Turnons: From a technical standpoint, the management team looks exceedingly well-suited for continued product development. Salaries for top-level managers are in the $100,000 range, and bonuses are in the $10,000 – $15,000 range, which is reasonable for a company in this situation.

Turnoffs: From a management, finance, and marketing standpoint, although certain individuals appear to have good credentials, we feel that there may be some gaps.

III. Financial Position

(Note: Revenue and income are reported in $000)	1987	1988	1989	% change '88–'89
Revenues	4,683	6,064	7,921	31%
Gross Profit	3,181	4,414	6,009	36%
Oper. Income	983	1,551	1,872	21%
NIAT	549	994	1,385	39%

Turnons: The company has no long-term debt and has about $4 million in cash and equivalents as well as a $1 million unsecured line of credit, from which it has never borrowed.

Turnoffs: A concern that we have with the company's balance sheet is the relatively high level of accounts receivable, which have grown at the rate of 83% over the past year, or nearly *three times* the rate of sales.

One concern regarding the company's accounting method for its revenues is that Integrated recognizes revenues from initial license agreements at the time that the product is shipped, rather than having revenues accrued as they are earned over the full year, which would be a more conservative approach.

IV. Financial Arrangement

	Shares Purchased # (000)	Shares Purchased %	Consideration Amt ($000)	Consideration %	Avg Price/ Share
Existing Investors	6,580	83%	$1,246	12%	$ 0.19
New Investors	1,350	17%	$9,113	88%	$ 6.75
TOTAL	7,930	100%	$10,359	100%	

Turnoffs: Our first concern regarding the financial arrangement is the use of the proceeds. The company states that the principal purposes of the offering are to increase working capital (which is a way of using long-term investment dollars to fund short-term operations) and to provide a public market for the company's stock (which will facilitate *cashing out* later by the existing shareholders). It is generally unclear exactly how the company plans to use the proceeds; top management has a lot of leeway in this regard.

There are several concerns regarding the *one-sidedness* of this financial arrangement, in which the officers and other insiders will benefit tremendously. After the offering, the officers, directors, and the venture capital firm that funded Integrated a few years ago will own over two-thirds of the equity of the company; the CEO and his wife will own nearly one-half of the venture.

At a total postoffering valuation of $54 million, the price appears high for a company like Integrated, whose revenues have not even reached $8 million per year. The valuation is almost 40 times earnings.

It should be noted that one-quarter of the 1.8 million shares offered are being sold by existing shareholders; this is a relatively high percentage.

Overall Analysis

In summary, we feel that Integrated Systems is a fairly solid company. The financials are strong. Management is adequate. We are, however, concerned with the financial arrangement; the company has not articulated clearly what it expects to do with the proceeds, aside from creating a public market for the stock itself; we do know that the officers and directors will realize very attractive profits once this company does go public. Nonetheless, this will likely be a better than average performer over the coming years. It may, however, take some time before the stock price reflects its true value.

READER'S DIGEST ASSOCIATION

I. Product/Market

Turnons: The *Reader's Digest* Association (RDA) has been selling its products in the United States since 1922 and in the international markets since 1938. Its customer list exceeds 50 million. RDA is one of the most experienced direct mail marketers in the world.

For a company generating nearly $2 billion per year in revenues, it is quite focused in its product line. Its major product, *Reader's Digest* magazine, enjoys significant competitive advantages due to its longstanding international reputation. Its other publications and home entertainment products face greater competition. Nonetheless, this is a company and an industry that can be quite attractive, largely because of the recurring revenues that it has been realizing and will likely realize over the coming years.

Turnoffs: As is typical of other established, 50-year old companies, RDA's growth has slowed considerably recently, to less than 10% per year over the last five years. Even this growth figure may be a bit inflated, as a substantial part of its increased revenues is a direct result of increased subscription prices, rather than of new subscriptions.

II. Management and Organization

Turnons: RDA has assembled a group of managers that is characteristic of many *Fortune* 500 companies. Most of the top level managers have 30 or more years of experience with RDA and have spent their entire careers with the company.

Turnoffs: Our biggest concern is that the management team and the directors are "too senior." They have experience, yet they may be lacking in innovative new approaches to guide the company over the long term.

Executive salaries for RDA officers are high—in the range of $1/2 million to $1 million per year (including bonuses) for the top level managers. However, for a $2 billion company, these salaries may be considered only "average size." The salaries, however, only tell part of the story. There are several incentive plans—including an incentive compensation plan, a long-term incentive plan (with stock options, stock appreciation rights, and so forth), a deferred compensation plan, a profit sharing plan, a retirement plan, a supplemental retirement plan, a severance plan, an income continuation plan, a stock purchase plan—which have provided millions of dollars more in cash and stock for top executives. Such lucrative incentive plans provided to executives who are nearing the end of their careers may work to the benefit of the executives who are planning for their retirement, to the detriment of the investors.

It should also be noted that the company is involved in various litigations and claims. The company believes that any liability from these lawsuits should not have a material effect on its financial condition.

III. Financial Position

(Note: Revenue and income are reported in $ Mill)				
	1987	1988	1989	% change '88–'89
Revenues	1,420	1,712	1,832	7%
Oper. Income	149	213	206	- 3%
NIAT	95	142	152	7%

Turnons: RDA has generally shown a *steady*—but far from phenomenal—increase in revenues over the past few years, increasing by an average of less than 10% per year, from $1.3 billion in 1984, $1.4 billion in 1987, $1.8 billion in 1989. Operating profit has increased much more dramatically (but erratically)—at an average rate of about 40% over the past 5 years—from $44 million in 1984 to $150 million in 1987 to $207 million in 1989.

RDA has a strong working capital position, with a current ratio of over 2:1. Also, over 40% of its current assets are in the form of cash and equivalents, which suggests a very liquid position. In fact, cash has increased by almost 60% over the past year while receivables have remained constant and inventories have increased by only 6% from 1988 to 1989.

In most respects, the balance sheet looks strong, with very little long-term debt and declining levels of current liabilities. Retained earnings for this established company were $440 million in June, 1989.

Turnoffs: One concern that we have is how the company has spent its money. The largest expenditure on assets over the past year (as well as in each of the last 3 years) was $150 million, which was invested in *marketable securities* and *short-term investments*. Less than $50 million was spent on capital expenditures and business acquisitions—i.e., expenditures on business growth and expansion. Thus, considerably more money was spent on nonbusiness related risk-free investments (primarily government and corporate fixed-income securities) than on activities related in any way to fostering the company's growth.

Unlike typical high-growth companies that reinvest excess funds in the business, RDA has paid sizable dividends to its investors.

IV. Financial Arrangement

	Shares Purchased # (000)	%	Consideration Amt ($000)	Avg Price/ Share
Existing Investors	75,000	75%		
New Investors	25,000	25%	$500,000	$20.00
TOTAL	100,000	100%		

Turnons: The offering appears to be an equitable arrangement for the new investors. Although the existing officers, directors, and other shareholders will still own 3/4 of the common stock of the company after the offering, the company seems to be fairly valued at approximately $2 billion (which equals 1.1 times revenues or 13 times after tax earnings for 1989) at its post offering time. Typically, companies in this industry have a market value of approximately 1 1/2 – 2 times revenues or 15 – 20 times earnings.

Turnoffs: There is always a concern when *all* the proceeds of an IPO are going to the selling shareholders, and not to the company, which is the case of RDA. However, in this particular case, the concern is *lessened* somewhat (but not eliminated) because the selling shareholders are charitable trusts, which are selling their shares largely because of changes in the tax law. .

Overall Analysis

It can be argued certainly that there's nothing too *exciting* about the *Reader's Digest* Association. RDA is merely a company with: a 50 year history; a strong and established product line; an *enormous* customer base; steady, but increasing revenues and earnings; and a well-respected management team. We are, however, concerned with the company's conservative, low-growth strategy, which may impact negatively on growth and expansion over the coming years.

Nonetheless, this company has one of the most recognizable products in the world that will likely continue to survive (but not excite us) over the years to come. For this reason, even though the company seems rather *fairly* valued at the time of its IPO, its popular appeal has the potential to push the stock price up by 10% or more shortly after its public offering. However, we would not expect the company to perform like a typical growth business after that; it is more likely to perform like any other high yield, dividend-oriented, stable company—*boring, but safe!* There are very few risks associated with this company. RDA appears to be a better than average investment value.

SULLIVAN DENTAL PRODUCTS

I. Product/Market

Turnons: Sullivan has a clearly defined product line and a focused market to which to sell its dental products. The company has managed to compete quite well against the more than 400 dealers and mail order companies in this industry and has established a fairly recognizable and reputable name over its 10-year history.

Turnoffs: Although Sullivan's sales have increased substantially over the past few years, the industry, as a whole, can hardly be characterized as "high growth," with unlimited opprtunities for expansion. In addition, the industry is highly competitive as well as price sensitive.

II. Management and Organization

Turnons: Sullivan has a few "industry veterans" at the top level of its organization, each of whom has 20–35 years of experience in the dental products industry.

Turnoffs: A concern is that the company has only two outside directors, who just happen to be a father and son lawyer team. We are not aware of any deficiencies that they have in terms of their skills. However, we feel that these directors, who are members of the law firm that represents Sullivan (and whose fees charged to Sullivan in 1990 represent more than 5% of the law firm's gross revenues), can hardly be referred to as independent, unbiased advisers to Sullivan who are the best-suited individuals to provide needed experience in the areas of management, marketing, and finance.

Sullivan has had some related party transactions with Dash Medical Gloves, Inc. (Dash), a corporation formed in 1988, and owned by the present stockholders of Sullivan.

III. Financial Position

(Note: Revenue and income are reported in $000)			
	1987	*1988*	*1989*	*% change '88–'89*
Revenues	15,655	25,023	34,639	38%
Gross Profit	4,758	7,667	10,811	41%
Oper Income	857	1,773	2,885	63%
NIAT	310	834	1,561	87%

Turnons: Sullivan has experienced substantial growth over the past few years, having grown by 4-fold since 1985. The vast majority of the sales growth is a result of increased *unit* sales, rather than of increases in price. Sales increased by 60% from 1987 to 1988 and by 38% from 1988 to 1989.

Profits have increased at even a faster rate than revenues. Gross and net margins, which were 31.2% and 4.5%, respectively, in 1989, were at their highest levels in recent years. Net income increased by 87% from 1988 to 1989.

Receivables and inventory grew at approximately the same rate as revenues, which is a healthy sign, and is indicative of controlled growth.

The debt position should not be considered alarming, as the company is generating enough cash from operations to more than cover its interest expense, as indicated by its interest coverage ratio of more than 5.0.

Turnoffs: The company's debt position, although having improved over the last 5 years, is still at over 70% of total assets. (Debt is almost all in the form of short-term payables, which will be wiped out with the proceeds from this offering.)

The company's liquidity position is of some concern to us. The quick ratio is only 0.5. In addition, the company had only $33,000 in cash at the end of 1989.

We also have a concern regarding Sullivan's cash flow position. The company had a large net cash outflow from operations in 1988. Over the past three years, cash flow from operations (CFFO) has not been large enough to cover net cash outflows for investing and financing activities. Consequently, the company had to borrow about $12 million (in short-term notes payable to banks) during that time to cover the shortfall in cash.

IV. Financial Arrangement

	Shares Purchased		Consideration	Avg Price/
	# (000)	%	Amt ($000)	Share
Existing Investors	2,475	74%		
New Investors	850	26%	$7,863	$9.25
TOTAL	3,325	100%		

Turnons: The $31 million postoffering valuation—which is approximately 0.9 times revenues, or 20 times earnings for 1989—appears fair for the new investor, considering that the company has been growing at a rapid rate and can continue to expand just as rapidly if the planned expansion goes as expected.

Turnoffs: A concern to us is that approximately 15% of the shares being offered are being sold by officers and directors.

Another concern, based on the information provided in the prospectus, is the absence of prior funding from established venture capital firms. We feel that companies which have gone through the private venture funding process, and who have established an arrangement with venture capital firms (which includes representation on the board of directors), are generally in a better position to emerge as superior performers following an initial public offering of stock than are companies that have not benefited from a venture capital relationship.

Overall Analysis

Sullivan has a clearly defined product and target market that has grown substantially in recent years. The company has a recognizable and respected name in the medical/dental field, which should enhance revenue growth and should make the company a fairly attractive investment opportunity. Its planned expansion, which will require about $2 million of the total proceeds raised, should enable the company to continue its growth—and, quite possibly, its returns for its investors—over the coming years.

There are concerns regarding the company's management/directors and its financial position—especially its debt and cash flows. However, overall, the risks are not uncontrollable. We feel that Sullivan has the potential to be a better than average performer over the forseeable future which, considering its low level of risk, should make Sullivan an attractive investment opportunity.

CHAPTER 10

Bumps ... and Bruises

- **Orbital Sciences**
- **Safeway Stores**

There are a few examples of new issues which demonstrate some substantial risks for the investor:

- Orbital Sciences
- Safeway Stores

The risks accompanying Orbital Sciences are evident upon a careful reading of its financial statements. Safeway is quite different in that it is a "reverse LBO" situation in which new investors are taking over substantial risks from the earlier stage investors in the company.

Although these companies might have some short-term stock price appreciation, we feel that they are more likely to lose value than gain value over the forseeable future. The risk/return characteristics of these investments do not appear attractive.

ORBITAL SCIENCES CORPORATION

I. Product/Market

Turnons: Orbital Sciences Corporation (Orbital) has been one of the fastest growing technology companies in the United States over the past five years, with sales skyrocketing from $174,000 in 1985 to $57 million in just the *first nine months* of 1989. The company has a backlog of over $150 million, thereby suggesting that sales growth is likely to continue.

Orbital's strategy is to become more focused than it has been on selected market segments of the space industry, which will likely give the company a competitive edge in the future. To expand its marketing, technical, and financial capabilities, Orbital has formed strategic business alliances with Martin Marietta, Hercules Inc., and Arianespace S. A.

Turnoffs: There may be tremendous growth potential for a company in this industry, especially since typical long-term government contracts for space products can be priced in the tens (or hundreds) of millions of dollars. The critical factor, however, is the government's future funding of the space program. If the funding continues, Orbital will likely benefit. However, if the funding dries up, then the smaller companies—like Orbital—will be the first ones to suffer.

II. Management and Organization

Turnons: Orbital appears to have a well-educated group of managers, who have earned degrees from such standout universities as Stanford, Cal Tech, MIT, and Harvard.

The management team is supported by a board with excellent credentials; the *ten* outside directors have corporate, military, political, and venture capital experience, all vital components for Orbital's success.

Turnoffs: Orbital's prospectus states that some of the officers owe the company $255,000, incurred in connection with the purchase of their general partnership interests in the limited partnership (presumably, such loans were made sometime around 1983 when the partnership was formed), and that the notes will be paid *in connection with* the liquidation of the limited partnership. This indicates that the insiders might be selling some of their equity stake either at this time or in the near future.

III. Financial Position

(Note: Revenue and income are reported in $000)

	1986	1987	1988	% change '87–'88
Revenues	3,676	25,295	35,089	39%
Gross Profit	2,482	3,943	2,713	-31%
Oper Income	1,175	-69	-6,600	NM
NIAT	4,540	206	-5,789	NM

Turnons: For the most part, Orbital's accounting practices are fairly conservative. In fact, the company amortized goodwill over just 20 years, rather than over the usual 40 years, which has the effect of actually *understating* net income by nearly $700,000 per year. This should be viewed positively by investors.

Turnoffs: Although revenues have increased steadily and dramatically, profitability has been erratic; Orbital has had net losses in every year with the exceptions of 1986 and 1987.

The most striking feature of Orbital's earnings statement has been its exceedingly low gross profit margins, which have actually been *negative* throughout most of its operating history. The gross margins are so low that it appears as if Orbital will have a difficult time making a profit, *regardless* of how much it can reduce its operating costs, which have more than doubled over the past year.

We are also concerned with several features of Orbital's balance sheet. Although long-term debt has been rather low, Orbital's current obligations are sizable and they have increased over the past year substantially.

Orbital has a major problem in its liquidity position; the company reported a deficit working capital of over $5 million as well as current and quick ratios of less than 1.0 in its most recent financials.

There are two other (possibly related) concerns regarding Orbital's financial statements. First, it should be noted that the company changed auditors from 1989 to 1990. Second, the auditor's report, dated February 4, 1990, reports data for the 9-month period ending September 30, 1989, rather than for the entire year.

IV. Financial Arrangement

| | Shares Purchased | | Consideration | | Avg Price/ Share |
	# (000)	%	Amt ($000)	%	
Existing Investors	8,036	87%	$49,628	73%	$ 6.18
New Investors	1,250	13%	$18,750	27%	$15.00
TOTAL	9,286	100%	$68,378	100%	

Turnons: Over the past few years, it appears as if Orbital has been quite successful at raising early stage capital.

Turnoffs: One important concern is that the limited partnership, which is Orbital's largest shareholder, will be selling 900,000 of its 4.1 million shares of stock when the company goes public.

Another concern regarding the financial arrangement is the use of proceeds. The company states that a principal purpose of the offering is to repay *short-term* debt. We view this practice of using long-term oriented funds to pay off short-term obligations very negatively, since the funds do not contribute necessarily to the long-term growth of the business.

Overall Analysis

Orbital has prepared a clear, easy-to-follow prospectus, which serves as an effective capsule summary of the company's current and planned financial position. There are some attractive features about Orbital. Most notably, this is a high-growth technology company, managed by some very educated and, presumably, motivated young managers, who can propel the stock price upwards. Nonetheless, we have some very serious question marks about the company. Of particular concern are the low gross margins and the poor liquidity position, both of which could result in weak earnings and in an unhealthy cash flow position over the years to come. The risks inherent in an investment in this company are substantial.

SAFEWAY

I. Product/Market

Turnons: Safeway operates in a highly competitive, price sensitive environment. Nonetheless, according to the company's prospectus, Safeway believes that it holds the number one or number two position in 18 of the 21 major metropolitan markets it serves.

Since 1987, the company has added 101 new stores and has remodeled 276 stores. Superstores, which have over 35,000 square feet, currently represent 44% of Safeway's stores, as compared to 35% of Safeway's stores at the beginning of 1987. Safeway has announced a $3.2 billion capital expenditure program of expansion and remodeling for the period 1990–1994. This is approximately double the amount of capital expenditures for the prior 5-year period. The funds will be used to build larger stores with more (higher margin) specialty departments, in order to increase the profitability of the company.

Turnoffs: Safeway's sales are down about 25% from their levels in 1985 and 1986 (i.e., prior to the LBO), due largely to the sell-off of stores.

II. Management and Organization

Turnons: Safeway has an experienced management team. The executive officers have served an *average* of 20 years, and its retail division managers an *average* of 33 years, with Safeway.

Turnoffs: The company has more than twenty executive officers, which seems a bit "top heavy," even for a company of this size. The company's prospectus provides very little information about their backgrounds, except to say that they have worked for Safeway for a while.

Executive salaries are high and bonuses can be as high as an officer's base salary. In 1989, a year in which the net worth of Safeway actually *declined* by over $20 million, *each* of the five highest paid officers (compensation data was presented for these five officers only) earned nearly as much in bonuses as in base salary. (Of course, that could be just reward for their performances; alternatively, these bonuses might have contributed to the company's 92% *decrease* in net income.) The chairman/CEO's total compensation was $1.2 million. The important point is, what is the purpose of an *incentive* compensation plan? If full bonuses are paid to each officer, regardless of the performance of the company, then what "incentive" do the executives have to improve performance? Such an incentive plan promotes complacency and does little to foster increased growth and profitability, which are linked directly to stock appreciation for the new investors of the company.

In addition to high salaries and bonuses, there are other attractive provisions for the executives that do not result necessarily in increased earnings for the company nor in higher returns for public investors. These include: lucrative consulting contracts upon retirement from the company, supplemental income payment during retirement, profit sharing plans, pension plans, severance pay in the case of a change of control in Safeway (which provides for a severance benefit of 299.99% of the officer's salary—they had to find a way to keep it under 300%, and 299.99% seemed like a convenient number), and a stock option plan. The stock option plan is, perhaps, the most attractive of these perks. Safeway has authorized the granting of 8 million shares of stock (remember, this entire offering is for 10 million shares). In *1989* alone, approximately 1 million of these options (which are worth about $15 million at the proposed IPO price) were granted at an exercise price of $2 per share (or about one-seventh to one-eighth of the offering price). As an example, the chairman/CEO, who has options to purchase 175,000 shares at $2 per share (that's about three months compensation for him), will realize approximately a $2.5 million gain (which, by the way, is roughly equal to Safeway's net profit for the year) on his stock just for options granted in 1989; he will realize another $13 million in profits when he exercises the remainder of his options.

Currently, Safeway has seven directors, two of whom are officers of the company and the remainder are associated with KKR (or the SSI Partnership, whose general partners are the general partners of KKR). In effect, the directors are all insiders, which is not at all what we would expect or want for a $14 billion company. Greater outsider representation on the board, which is designed to protect the interests of the stockholders (particularly the new public investors, rather than only KKR and the management investors), is useful in monitoring incentive compensation plans—like the one just described—which are great for the executives receiving the bonuses, but not necessarily for the outside stockholders of the company.

It should be noted that Safeway has paid KKR approximately $2 million in management fees over the past 3 years. Of course, this is a relatively small amount, compared to the $1 billion or so postoffering equity position that KKR will have in Safeway; that's not bad for their *$175 million* investment which was made three years ago.

It should also be noted that there are and have been several legal proceedings against Safeway, some of which have been settled recently. One case involves a class action suit on behalf of 210 employees which alleges wrongful termination shortly after the LBO. There has been a settlement agreement, which is now subject to court approval. There is also a suit arising out of a fire at a Safeway warehouse as well as several lawsuits arising from the normal course of Safeway's business.

III. Financial Position

(Note: Revenue and income are reported in $ Mill)				
	1987	*1988*	*1989*	*% change '88-'89*
Revenues	18,301	13,612	14,325	5%
Gross Profit	4,542	3,436	3,690	7%
Oper. Income	417	326	462	42%
NIAT	-488	32	3	-92%

Turnons: Although Safeway's sales are down considerably from its pre-LBO days, the company just experienced its first year of growth since the LBO—a 5% *increase* in sales from 1988 to 1989, following a 20% *decrease* in sales from 1987 to 1988.

Gross margins have been in the 25% range consistently—which is respectable for this industry—and have, in fact, been rising slightly, but steadily, over the past few years. The increase in gross margins is due partly to Safeway's greater attention to specialty departments, which have higher margins than other departments.

There are some interesting points that relate to the company's operating margin and net profit margin over the past two years. From 1988 to 1989, while sales increased by 5%, operating income increased by 42%, but net income *decreased* by 92%. Why? This difference in net income from 1988 to 1989 was due to: a one-time gain of $48 million on the sale of assets in 1988; and a rather hefty tax bill in 1989 (of $91.5 million on $94 million of operating income, an increase of 900% from the previous year). It appears as if Safeway had some tax credits due to losses in 1987 and 1988, which have since been used up. Consequently, the "bottom line" makes Safeway's earnings in 1989 (as compared to 1988) appear worse than they were in actuality.

There are some important performance measures for retailers that are worth noting. First, the average weekly sales per store and the average weekly sales per square foot have increased by approximately 9% and 7%, respectively, over each of the past 3 years. These increases may be due to a large extent on the merchandise carried by the newer, larger stores that the company has opened, rather than due to greater efficiencies of operation of existing stores; this is supported by the fact that the average sales percentage increases have been less than 6% over the past three years.

Turnoffs: Operating margins have been in the 2% range, which although low, is fairly typical of grocery retailers. The company has had a very small net profit in 1988 and 1989, after having had net losses in the prior 2 years. In 1989, net income was $2.5 million (on sales of over $14 billion), which was about twice the total compensation (excluding stock options) of Peter Magowan, the company's chairman/CEO.

A very important concern is that, due to Safeway's high debt position, its interest coverage ratio is approximately 1.0 (i.e., its interest expense is approximately equal to its operating income). This figure is quite low, and is indicative of the company having potential problems in covering its debt payments. Interestingly, Safeway plans to finance a portion of its $3.2 billion expansion from operating income. The company may be overly optimistic in this regard as there is barely enough operating income—at current levels—to finance its *interest* payments alone, which were $383 million in 1989. In fact, 1989 was the first year since the LBO where Safeway's operating income exceeded its interest expense.

An examination of Safeway's balance sheet shows that, from 1988 to 1989, cash *increased* and accounts receivables *decreased*, both by about 30%. This would be fine by itself. However, we have a major concern with Safeway's overall liquidity position; Safeway has a *deficit* working capital—or a current ratio of less than 1.0—that has become increasingly negative over the past few years, to its present level of *negative* $215 million. Safeway's quick ratio is an alarmingly low 0.16, which indicates that most of the company's short term assets are in the form of inventory. (Let's hope that not too much of it is in the produce or dairy sections.)

Safeway's debt position, as would be expected for a recent LBO, is far from ideal. Total liabilities are greater than total assets—i.e., the company has a *deficit* stockholders' equity, which has decreased from *positive* $1.6 billion in 1985 to *negative* $389 million today.

Safeway's unused borrowing capacity is $475 million under bank credit agreements. The company feels that this is adequate to meet the company's requirements. However, it should be noted that Safeway currently has $3.1 billion in debt outstanding, with $1 billion of indebtedness to mature over the next five years. The current debt position already provides significant strains on the company's cash flow position. In fact, according to the company's prospectus:

> If future cash provided by operations is less than that realized since the [LBO], Safeway may experience difficulty meeting the interest and principal payments due on outstanding indebtedness, rent, and other obligations.

There are restrictions placed upon Safeway due to its heavy debt burden. Specifically, the bank credit agreements limit or prohibit Safeway from paying dividends, incurring additional indebtedness, disposing of material amounts of assets, and so forth. Thus, unlike most stable-growth oriented retailers, upon which investors can at least count on periodic dividends, investors in Safeway will likely benefit only from significant increases in the price of the stock.

There is one more note of interest which involves Safeway's "creative accounting" practices. Over the first three quarters of the past two years, the company has shown fairly steady net *profits* in just about each of these quarters; however, in the last quarter of the year, Safeway reported sizable net *losses*. In 1989, for example, Safeway's profits were $8.8 million, $7.7 million, and $7.1 million over the first three quarters; yet, the company had net *losses* of $21.1 million in the fourth quarter. Clearly, this industry is not so cyclical from quarter to quarter to justify these uneven earnings. A more likely explanation is that Safeway follows the "big bath theory"—i.e., the company writes off losses at the most opportune time. The reason that it is opportune to write off losses in the fourth quarter is that companies file quarterly 10–K reports with the SEC for the first three quarters, but, instead of filing a 10–K for the fourth quarter, they file an *annual* 10–K with the SEC; thus, companies will sometimes wait until the fourth quarter to take substantial losses since fourth quarter performance is not reported by itself, but, rather, is combined with the other three quarters for a year end report.

IV. Financial Arrangement

Turnoffs: Safeway is a classic case of how LBO artists, like KKR, can benefit from such deals handsomely. KKR and its affiliate, SSI Partners, acquired the then publicly held Safeway in 1986. Their initial investment was a mere $175 million (plus the company's assumption of $5.8 billion in debt). KKR then sold about half of Safeway's stores, thus cutting Safeway's debt to a more palatable $3.1 billion. At a proposed offering price of $15 per share, the public's 10 million shares will bring in $150 million for about 10% of the equity of the company. This is almost as much as the $175 million that KKR invested three years ago for *100%* of the equity in Safeway. That's a fairly attractive return for KKR, considering that the company's sales, profits, assets, and net worth are lower substantially (while debt, of course, is higher substantially) than they were when KKR took over the company. The public investors can only grin, since that's simply the nature of LBO deals. (Of course, it doesn't always work out so nicely, as evidenced by the recent failures of Campeau and Jim Walter.)

An important concern is—*why* is Safeway planning to go public? That is, what will the company do with $150 million in proceeds? On the surface, it might look attractive. There is nothing mentioned in the prospectus about KKR or members of Safeway's management team having plans to cash out at the time of the offering; thus, all proceeds will go to the company. Moreover, according to the prospectus, Safeway plans to use the proceeds from this offering for capital expenditures, including its planned expansion; this would be an appropriate use of proceeds. However, the IPO will provide about 5% of the $3.2 billion needed for the expansion. From where will the remaining $3 billion come? The company claims that part of the funding will come from operations. However, as just discussed, income from operations has barely—if at all—covered interest expenses. Another possible source of funding would be debt financing. However, as noted earlier, there are provisions in the bank credit agreements which limit the amount of debt of the company; the last thing that Safeway needs at this time is additional debt. Of course, another source of funding is a secondary stock offering; by that time there may be more sellers than buyers, which could adversely affect the price of the stock. The important point is that Safeway's current cash position will not enable it to achieve its planned level of financing; we have adhered generally to a position of caution for companies whose financing needs are so great that the funds generated through an IPO are a small fraction of what they'll need over the next 2 – 5 years of its operations.

Safeway's postoffering valuation will be about $1.5 billion, which equals approximately 10% of its sales revenues or three times its operating profits; that would indicate a rather fair valuation. However, it should be noted that the public investors will be paying substantially more for their stock than: the holders of merger warrants, who, in November, 1986, were granted the rights to acquire 4.6 million shares at a price of $3.80 per share; the holders of the SSI Partnership warrants (whose general partners just happen to be the partners in KKR), who were granted the rights to purchase 13.9 million shares of stock at $2 per share; and the management investors, who currently hold warrants to purchase 7 million shares of stock at $2 per share. The questions for the investor are: Did KKR and the existing management team increase the stock's value by 7- or 8-fold over the past few years? Is KKR likely to further increase the stock's value substantially once a public market for the stock exists?

Overall Analysis

In many respects, this is not a company that should go public. The financial arrangement is structured around what is best for KKR and the officers of Safeway, rather than around what is best for the new stockholders in the company, who will, after all, own only 10% of the common stock (or much less after the exercise of several million outstanding options or options to be granted). In fact, with the "public" owning only 10% of the stock, why should this even be called a "public" offering? In actuality, it is a "privately" held multibillion dollar company that will just happen to have a few public investors. If the purpose of the offering is to raise $150 million—which will hardly be enough to cover its planned expansion—then why doesn't Safeway seek funding from one of the dozens of large, cash-rich corporations who would be glad to invest in such a company? Perhaps the reason is that this offering creates a public market for the stock. This should be viewed with extreme caution by the investor, as it provides an opportunity for the existing shareholders to sell a portion of their stock positions in the aftermarket. Of course, we would not expect KKR to sell a large percentage of its 65 million shares of stock, since that would cause a major decline in the price of the stock. It would also be ridiculous to expect KKR (or any other corporate raider) to launch a takeover bid on Safeway that would cause the stock price to rise dramatically, since KKR will already own 80% of the company *after* this offering.

Certainly, Safeway has the potential to be a steady—but probably not a superior—performer over the coming years. Moreover, it is in too stable a position to come crashing down in value. However, the deal structure is one that favors the existing stockholders and the management team much more than the new public investors. Unlike other recent large IPOs (for example, *Reader's Digest*), that offer attractive dividends as well as *significant* upside potential in the value of their stock to investors, we would expect very little movement—and more likely downward movement than upward movement—in the price of the stock as long as the current conditions for the company persist.

CHAPTER 11

The "Losers"

- **Brooksfilms**
- **Cellular Information Systems**
- **Digital Sound Corporation**
- **Xenejenex**

Of the ten companies that we categorized, we rated four of them as clear "losers," based on their risk/return characteristics. They include:

- Brooksfilms
- Cellular Information Systems
- Digital Sound Corp.
- Xenejenex

Two of the companies—Cellular and Xenejenex—are early stage ventures that we feel are going public prematurely. Digital has some significant risks associated with it due to its competitive position. And Brooksfilms is a company that has been around for awhile, but seems to be tapping the public markets for the wrong reasons. As such, they are all risky investment opportunities that have only limited upside potential.

BROOKSFILMS

I. Product/Market

Turnons: Mel Brooks' experience with the motion picture and television industry is a vital component of the company's long-term success.

II. Management and Organization

Turnoffs: The Brooksfilms' executives are hardly indicative of a professional "management team." Although we are not in a position to judge the capabilities of these individuals—and it appears that *some* of these executives may have the appropriate experience to manage this company—the management team is composed largely of individuals with backgrounds in law, accounting, and investment banking, who are, in some cases, working on a part-time basis, while drawing lucrative salaries.

There are some other concerns regarding specific managers of the company. One of the executives and one of the directors—both of whom are attorneys—have been upper-level managers with companies that have gone bankrupt. The director (who has the dubious distinction of being involved in two companies that have gone bankrupt), was CEO of DeLaurentiis Entertainment, a financial disaster.

III. Financial Position

(Note: Revenue and income are reported in $000)			
	1987	*1988*	*1989*	*% change '88–'89*
Revenues	2,683	4,608	6,549	42%
Oper. Income	-1,877	3,803	4,813	27%
NIAT	-1,803	407	323	-21%

Turnons: The company has a strong working capital position and a favorable debt position, with almost $3 million in cash and about $1 million in *total* liabilities.

Turnoffs: Brooksfilms' revenues have declined steadily and dramatically, from $6 million in 1985 to less than $3 million in 1987. Revenues have begun to increase over the last two years to their most recent level of about $6.5 million.

Earnings have also been unsteady over this period, with a net loss of nearly $2 million in 1987 (which was largely a result of a $4.4 million amortization of film costs), and net profits of between $250 million and $400 million in the other four years. The unevenness of revenues and profits is dictated largely by the production schedules and the success of a given motion picture. Thus, it's likely that the same pattern of uneven revenues and profits will appear in the future.

Its cash position is such that the company has earned more in interest income over the first 6 months of fiscal 1990 than it has in license fees. This concerns us: What business is Brooksfilms in? What revenues (that is, how much and from what source) can we expect from Brooksfilms over the next few years?

IV. Financial Arrangement

| | Shares Purchased | | Consideration | | Avg Price/ |
	# (000)	%	Amt ($000)	%	Share
Existing Investors	3,000	67%	$ 2	0%	$ 0.01
New Investors	1,500	33%	$15,000	100%	$10.00
TOTAL	4,500	100%	$15,002	100%	

Turnoffs: As demonstrated above, Brooksfilms is being valued at approximately 7 times revenues and 140 times earnings (for 1989). This seems exceedingly overpriced for a company that could not even be classified as a growth business. Another important concern is the disproportionate investment of the existing as compared to the new investors in the business. The existing investors have only invested $2,000 for 2/3 of the company. The new investors would have to invest $15 million for only 1/3 of the business. In terms of equity dilution, the new investors would be responsible for increasing the net tangible book value per share by 300%—from $.90 to $3.57. In short, the $45 million valuation of the company after the IPO (which would give Mr. Brooks nearly $30 million in equity for an insignificant financial investment) cannot be supported, given its unsteady level of revenues and its insignificant revenues and earnings growth over the last 5 years.

Overall Analysis

Mr. Brooks is an extremely funny individual—very likely, the funniest person in Hollywood. It is, therefore, very fitting that he put together a *very* funny deal. There are substantial risks associated with such a venture, with the expected returns not commensurate with those risks.

There is little justification for the $45 million valuation of the company. The proposed ownership arrangement appears quite inequitable for the new investor.

The authors of this book have been longtime fans of Mr. Brooks (having each seen *Blazing Saddles* a dozen times) and eagerly await the opening of his next film *Life Stinks*. We will certainly continue to be fans of Mel Brooks after this public offering. We'd be much bigger fans with a less comical offering.

CELLULAR INFORMATION SYSTEMS

I. Product/Market

Turnons: One very attractive feature of the nature of the company's service is the opportunity for (monthly) recurring revenues from cellular telephone subscribers.

Turnoffs: A big concern is whether Cellular can continue to grow in and dominate small regional markets (which is where Cellular operates). It is questionable whether there is something so special about Cellular—i.e., a significant competitive advantage—that limits the ability of its existing and potential competitors to pose a significant threat to Cellular. There are numerous established competitors—for example, GTE Mobilnet, McCaw Cellular, Centel, and Contel—which have strong managerial teams, substantial assets, and extensive experience in telecommunications who are much better positioned than Cellular to dominate such markets. Moreover, there is uncertainty as to the commercial feasibility of cellular telephone systems in small regional markets, be it by Cellular or any other competitor. Demand for the company's services is still uncertain.

Plus, Cellular has only been operating for the past 2 years.

II. Management and Organization

Turnons: Cellular might have some political clout, as evidenced by the company having former Senator Lowell Weicker (Conn.) on their board of directors.

Turnoffs: Based on the company's prospectus, there is little evidence to suggest that Cellular has a well-developed management team with appropriate experience in the telecommunications industry.

Compensation for the two top executives is $300,000 (plus lucrative stock options to an already attractive equity stake in the company), which is excessive for a $5 million company with such a tenuous cash flow position.

Several of the key executives of the company have significant other business interests and are, therefore, not devoting full time to this venture.

It should also be noted that certain stockholders and directors have charged the company nearly $1/2 million over the 1986–1988 period for legal and accounting services, through the professional firms in which they have an interest.

Another concern is the structure of the company. Cellular is a holding company, with its cellular interests owned through subsidiaries and through partnerships that it controls. This can result in related party transactions that could be more attractive to Cellular or CHI, than to the investors in Cellular.

III. Financial Position

(Note: Revenue and income are reported in $000)			
	1988	*1989*	*% change 88–'89*
Revenues	754	4,881	547%
Oper Income	–2,756	–7,688	NM
NIAT	–2,740	–11,097	NM

Turnoffs: The company has experienced cumulative net losses of $15.8 million through September 30, 1989 and expects to continue to incur losses at least through the end of 1992.

Of greater concern to us is the tenuous financial position and the growing cash needs of the company. An examination of the company's cash flow statement reveals that, as would be expected, Cellular's net cash flow position as a result of its operations was at a deficit point of nearly $12 million.

One more important note regarding the financials: The prospectus included an audit report for 1988, but only a review report for the 9 months ending September 30, 1989. We caution that the financial statements for the latter period are *unaudited*, thereby enhancing the risk of such an offering.

IV. Financial Arrangement

	Shares Purchased		Consideration		Avg Price/
	# (000)	%	Amt ($000)	%	Share
Existing Investors	5,693	67%	$ 4,643	13%	$ 0.82
New Investors	2,800	33%	$30,100	87%	$10.75
TOTAL	8,493	100%	$34,743	100%	

Turnoffs: Cellular will be using the proceeds from the IPO to repay bank indebtedness (rather than to fund future growth). We have always been cautious of such a financial arrangement, as it merely transfers the financial risks from the company to the outside investors. Related to this is the concern that we see continued debt mounting for the company, with long-term debt and stock being used to pay off short-term obligations.

There are risks associated with the nature of the financial arrangement. Specifically, the existing shareholders have contributed only $4.6 million of capital (or 13%), but will retain two-thirds of the ownership of the company.

Overall Analysis

In summary, we have several concerns regarding the investment value of Cellular. The service idea has potential, although Cellular's operating history is rather brief. We see little evidence of significant competitive advantages nor of appropriately experienced full-time, committed managers to give us the impression that Cellular will be a stellar performer over the coming years. The debt position of the company is alarming to us. Moreover, we have concerns with the apparent inequitable stock arrangement of this offering. The potential returns do not seem to be commensurate with potential risks.

We feel that an IPO at this time may be premature. According to the company's prospectus, Cellular has substantial cash needs at this time and will have even more needs over the coming years. Most of the cash is targeted towards repayment of debt. For Cellular, going public will provide the company with the infusion of cash that it needs. For the investor, the benefits are less obvious. This is a deal that investors would be best advised to pass up.

DIGITAL SOUND

I. Product/Market

Turnons: Digital Sound Corporation (Digital) has an established product and customer base.

Turnoffs: The company is part of an industry that is characterized by frequent and rapid changes in technology and intense competition, with most of the competitors being much larger than Digital. Although we are not in a position to judge the quality of Digital's line of products versus those of each of its major competitors, we are in a position to assess the company's relative competitive position. We have some serious concerns about Digital, relative to its competitors. Digital's competitors include: Octel, ROLM, AT&T, Northern Telecom, and VMX, depending upon which product lines are involved. They have much greater resources than Digital and can offer more than can Digital.

Digital has no patent protection for its existing products. In addition, Digital's manufacturing operations consist primarily of final assembly and testing of subassemblies and systems. Subcontractors do the balance of work. First, this makes Digital very dependent on the subcontractors. Second, this demonstrates that numerous other companies can do just what Digital is doing, and can create competitive advantages over Digital.

Another significant competitive weakness is that 65% of Digital's sales come from only four customers and nearly 90% of sales come from just ten customers. In fact, the largest customers have become even larger on a percentage basis this past year than they were previously.

In most respects, there are very few competitive advantages that Digital possesses over other companies, and several that others possess over Digital.

II. Management and Organization

Turnons: Digital benefits from having three directors from the venture capital/investment industry and one director who is an executive with Xerox.

Turnoffs: The management team is rather new to Digital. Four of the company's six executive officers have joined the company during the last 18 months.

Compensation seems somewhat high for a company that just became profitable. Specifically, the CEO earned over $300,000 last year and the senior VP earned close to $200,000. But compensation tells only part of the story. A concern is that several managers who have been with the company for just a year or two have lucrative stock options, which dilute the equity position of the new investors.

In October, 1989, a suit was filed against Systems Marketing Co., a leasing company, and Digital, alleging causes of action for misrepresentation in connection with the sale and lease of certain of Digital's products.

III. Financial Position

(Note: Revenue and income are reported in $000)				
	1987	1988	1989 '	% change 88–'89
Revenues	6,039	10,582	28,039	165%
Gross Profit	1,891	4,899	15,732	221%
Oper Income	-5,712	-5,501	4,332	NM
NIAT	-5,992	-5,735	4,007	NM

Turnons: According to the income statement, revenues for Digital have increased 14-fold from 1986 to 1989, with revenues nearly tripling from 1988 to 1989. This has been attributable to a large extent on the introduction of two new voice processing models that are more expensive (and more profitable) than the company's previous units.

In the realm of profitability, gross margins have been increasing as well, at an even greater rate than have revenues, due partly to the introduction of the new models. Gross margins for 1989 were 56%, up from 46% in 1988 and 36% in 1987.

Turnoffs: We have always maintained a cautious position on companies that go public immediately after their first profitable year (or quarter).

There is a possibility for significant fluctuations in the sales and profits of the company over the coming years due to the nature of its product line. The company sells voice processing equipment that can cost up to $1 million for a unit. Thus, a small number of orders can be significant for a company that earned $4 million on only $28 million in sales last year. There is little in the way of predictability, and little chance of recurring revenues from its customer base as a whole.

The company has had a problem relating to liquidity. The company did not generate any net cash from operating activities through the end of 1988, and barely generated cash from operations in 1989. During this entire time, the company has financed its excess cash needs from operations through short-term bank borrowings under a line of credit agreement.

IV. Financial Arrangement

| | Shares Purchased | | Consideration | | Avg Price/ |
	# (000)	%	Amt ($000)	%	Share
Existing Investors	13,327	84%	$38,201	68%	$2.87
New Investors	2,500	16%	$18,125	32%	$7.25
TOTAL	15,827	100%	$56,326	100%	

Turnons: Digital has been able to attract venture capital investments from such highly regarded firms as: Oak Investment Partners; Montgomery Securities; and Brentwood Associates. In addition, it should be noted that these investors are retaining all their stock shares in Digital. These should both be viewed as positive signs.

Turnoffs: According to its prospectus, Digital plans to use the funds to repay notes payable (Digital currently has a balance of $3.2 million on these notes) and the remainder for general corporate purposes. First, by paying off these notes, the company is transferring the risk from its present stockholders to the new investors. Second, we are concerned with the large amount of discretion that management has in spending the money from this offering. We would prefer that the company be more specific as to the use of its funds.

Some sophisticated early investors—Welsh Carson Anderson & Stowe; Saugatuck Capital; GE Pension Fund; Olivetti Partners—are selling sizable portions of their stock at the time of this offering, which should not be viewed positively.

The postoffering valuation is $115 million, which translates into 4 times revenues, or 48 times income before extraordinary items, or 29 times net income. This should be considered overvalued significantly for a company that has been a *mediocre* performer for *most* of its operating history (although last year was a strong year) and has an uncertain future.

Overall Analysis

In summary, we have several concerns regarding the investment value of Digital. Perhaps the sophisticated investors who are retaining their shares know something special about the company. However, our feeling is that there is nothing special about Digital that should justify such a high valuation. True, there is a need for its products. However, numerous competitors can provide them, which puts Digital in a precarious competitive position. The financial position of Digital, although attractive for 1989, has not demonstrated that the company is likely to be a stellar performer over the coming years. Of course, a technology oriented company like Digital has the potential to make significant upwards *and* downwards movements in its stock price, either immediately after its IPO, or at a later time. However, over the long term, we expect that Digital will perform at a below average level.

XENEJENEX

I. Product/Market

Turnons: Xenejenex has a focused product line.

Turnoffs: Xenejenex is a one-year old company. Moreover, it is a player in a very competitive industry consisting of numerous small businesses—like itself—that can enter the market easily due to the lack of barriers of entry, as well as several larger, more established businesses with substantial resources.

Xenejenex sells an extremely price-sensitive product, which, at a list price of about $25, makes it very difficult for the company to realize attractive profit margins.

There is uncertainty over the general nature of the industry; videotapes that address "special interests" such as health care and related topics are still at an early stage of development with a very uncertain future.

II. Management and Organization

Turnons: The management and directors of the company have outstanding academic credentials; these five individuals hold five academic degrees from Harvard (including two MBAs who were Baker scholars), as well as advanced degrees from other first rate programs. They are also well-trained in the financial aspects of the business and have links with the financial community.

Turnoffs: It is questionable whether the management team has the necessary experience in the operations of such a venture. In addition, there is an absence of individuals with lengthy tenures with established, or even growth businesses.

III. Financial Position

Turnons: The company has over $400,000 in working capital, as a result of its latest stock issuance, and a current ratio of about 5:1.

Receivables are only 5% of revenues, which suggests that either their customers are paying on time or their sales are on a cash basis primarily.

Turnoffs: The company anticipates continuing losses from operations as it expands its product line of videotapes over the coming years. We are concerned that the company is going public as such an early stage venture. This suggests a high degree of risk for the investor.

Based on the company's prospectus, we do not envision the videotape sales to become a very profitable part of the business, as long as the company continues with its current pricing strategy. Given the channels of distribution that are appropriate for this product, there is very little room for profit if the "suggested retail price" per unit is $25.

IV. Financial Arrangement

| | Shares Purchased | | Consideration | | Avg Price/ |
	# (000)	%	Amt ($000)	%	Share
Existing Investors	750	56%	$ 823	22%	$1.10
New Investors	600	44%	$ 3,000	78%	$5.00
TOTAL	1,350	100%	$ 3,823	100%	

Turnons: Bridger, currently the largest shareholder in the company, plans to purchase 150,000 additional shares of stock at the time of the offering. This is a very positive sign, since it shows that established investors who are very well aware of the company feel that the company's value will increase substantially over the coming years.

Turnoffs: A major concern that we have is the postoffering valuation of $6.75 million for a company that is *only one year old* and has generated a net loss of over $250,000 on revenues of $288,000 in its most recent year. The valuation translates into 23 times revenues for the most recent year (and 17 times current annualized revenues), which is an *exceedingly high* multiple for an unproven company that is not engaged in breakthrough technological research.

Overall Analysis

In summary, we have several concerns regarding the investment value of Xenejenex. Although the product idea has some appeal and the management team appears adequate, the company is still in the start-up phase, having completed just one year of operation. Moreover, the offering price seems high at 23 times revenues.

There are two key questions: 1. Will they generate substantial revenues in the future? 2. Will they do so profitably? It's difficult to answer these questions. Nobody can project sales growth of such an early stage venture accurately. That makes this offering exceedingly risky. Moreover, even if they *can* generate revenues, the current profit margins—especially for videotape sales—are simply not very attractive. Unfortunately, there's not too much—other than increasing sales dramatically—that the company can do to improve its margins for videotape sales since there is a maximum purchase price for the tapes (and the company may have already reached that level) and that there is a minimum production cost to ensure a quality product.

Nobody would be more pleased than us to see our hero, Mickey Mantle (who is featured in the company's *Feeling Good With Arthritis* videotape), reach stardom again. However, Xenejenex is simply not ready for the major leagues at this time. In essence, an IPO at this time may be premature. We do not envision a significant increase in its stock price and feel that the risk/return tradeoff would not make this an attractive investment opportunity.

PART FOUR

Putting It All Together

CHAPTER 12   Summary of Checklists

CHAPTER 12

Summary of Checklists

PRODUCT/MARKET: SUMMARY POINTS

- Look for companies that have a clearly defined focus ...
- ...But watch out for ones with too narrow a focus
- Look for companies that take advantage of social and demographic trends
- Cherish a company with a proprietary technology
- The absence of competitive advantages spells disaster
- Companies that spot trends early have a tremendous competitive advantage
- Proper timing plays an important role
- Look for companies with high quality products
- Low-tech companies can have significant competitive advantages
- Look for companies that are pioneers in an industry
- Beware of "hot" stocks in "hot" industries
- Be cautious...if growth seems unreal, it may be!
- High growth is sometimes an indicator of potential problems
- Look for an established track record of success
- Be cautious of early stage ventures
- A competitive edge: Developing a strong link with customers
- Be cautious of companies that are overly dependent upon a few large customers
- Be cautious of companies with a poor relationship with suppliers
- Riding the growth curve of customers enhances a company's value

MANAGEMENT AND ORGANIZATION: SUMMARY POINTS

- Management is more important than the technology
- Watch for omissions in the prospectus
- Beware of gaps in management teams
- Be wary of founders who lack experience and maturity
- Look for a full-time commitment in management
- Look for modest compensation packages
- Beware of "fat-cat" managers with huge bonuses
- Managers should own stock; when they benefit from their stock rising, so do investors
- Be wary of nepotism ...
- ...Although some families can work well together
- Look for a strong board of directors
- Prominent venture capitalists as directors can strengthen the company significantly
- Directors should add something valuable; otherwise, why have outside directors?
- Beware of companies offering its executives interest-free loans
- Watch for leases to related parties
- Beware of transactions that are not "silky" smooth
- Watch for any associations with shady characters
- Watch for quality and quantity of related party transactions
- Beware of pending litigation when the dollar amount is large
- Beware of pending litigation of a very serious nature

FINANCIAL STATEMENT ANALYSIS: SUMMARY POINTS

- Search for companies with strong earnings and earnings growth
- As earnings increase, so does the stock price in most cases
- Carefully monitor the P–E ratio
- Look beyond net income; beware of shrinking profit margins
- Look for "quality of earnings"
- Be careful of companies that use aggressive accounting practices such as front-end loading or smoothing of profits
- Use the balance sheet to predict future earnings
- Look for companies with ample liquidity
- Watch for unusual or unexplained increases in accounts receivable or inventory
- Watch for companies that manipulate inventory
- Watch for companies using aggressive inventory valuation
- Watch for bloated inventories
- Be attentive to insufficient solvency
- Monitor the debt/equity ratio
- Be aware of the problem with bank debt
- Be cautious of companies that fail to generate enough cash to fuel their growth
- Look for companies with strong cash flows from operations
- Look for companies with a cash management plan in effect
- Search for companies with strong cost controls in place
- Watch for audit reports with qualified opinions ... especially "going concern" qualifications
- Look for the absence of recent, audited financial statements
- Watch for changes in or disagreements with auditors
- Read the footnotes: look for conservative accounting policies

FINANCIAL ARRANGEMENT: SUMMARY POINTS

- Search for companies that use the proceeds from an offering to foster future growth
- Be cautious when funding is targeted for working capital
- Beware of companies that use funding to repay debt ...
- ...But, in some cases, using the proceeds to reduce debt is desirable
- Be cautious of selling shareholders
- Look for companies that have already received substantial funding, especially from established venture capitalists
- Be wary of companies that were turned down for funding previously
- Valuing high flyers requires more creativity
- Not all fast-growth, high-tech companies have excessive valuations
- Watch for those companies with outrageous valuations
- Look for substantial investments made by existing shareholders
- Consider the quality of the underwriter

Subject Index

Company Index